THE GREAT LIBERAL DEATH WISH

PAUL J. DELMONT

FOUR WAYS THE POLITICAL ESTABLISHMENT IS FAILING AMERICA

ISBN 978-1475065619

Cover art by Hadar Naftalovich
Cover coloring by Paul Summerfield (www.ageofwonder.org)
Cover design and book typesetting by Michelle Lovi (www.odysseybooks.com.au)

This book is dedicated to the memory of:

William F. Buckley, Jr.,
who first encouraged this project

and to

Malcolm Muggeridge,
whose warnings decades ago are timely today

CONTENTS

INTRODUCTION

America is in crisis today – a crisis of confidence and of leadership. The spread of nuclear weapons will very shortly be an existential threat not only to smaller democracies, such as South Korea and Israel, but to the United States and the democracies of Europe as well. More rogue regimes may profit from this dramatic change of fortune, as may terrorists.

The American presidency has deteriorated into a media circus and Barack Obama has spent fully half of his first term running for reelection to a second. Critical of corporate jet use, he employs the biggest corporate jet of all (funded by taxpayers) for his own political use and the interests of his party. Obama was elected because of his skills at campaigning and public oratory and not much else, a reflection of our seriously flawed primary/debate system for nominating presidential candidates. Obama postures, while avoiding real challenges, pushing an agenda that makes America weak and financially at risk and on the road to semi-socialism. Most amazing of all, as the nuclear missile threat grows exponentially, Obama and his Democratic Party call for cutting back U.S. missile defense systems.

As president, Obama has failed to deal with the four long-term crises described in this book: the irrational way we

1

nominate presidential candidates, amounting to politics as entertainment; out of control immigration, which threatens the survival of the two party system; the arrogant assumption by courts of legislative powers reserved to Congress, and the proliferation of nuclear weapons to hostile dictatorships. Obama has been equally ineffective in dealing with a fifth: government bankruptcy. The Great Recession caused deep cuts in government income at all levels and the federal – and many state and local governments – are deeply in debt. Jefferson County, Alabama (which includes Birmingham, a metro area of a half million people), has filed bankruptcy on debts running over $3 billion. Harrisburg, Pennsylvania, has also filed bankruptcy. California is on the brink and Federal debt is spiraling out of control, with trillion dollar deficits forecast for a decade or longer. Federal government debt could reach 200% of GNP relatively soon.

Liberals like Obama have no answers other than adding to debt-funded government outlays. Obama, as noted, has failed to address the building of nuclear weapons by dictators, a development that threatens not only the democracies, but the environment and economics of the entire planet. Obama's dysfunction has been matched by that of Congress, now held in contempt by a vast majority of Americans. Unable to pass sensible long or short term spending cuts, or to adjust taxation and revenues in this crisis, the Democrat-dominated Senate and the Republican-dominated House of Representatives passed their responsibilities on to a Congressional "Super Committee," which became predictably deadlocked and ineffectual. A long run of failed or mediocre presidents, extending back to Kennedy and Nixon, combined with increasingly dysfunctional Congresses, has created a leadership crisis at the highest level of American government.

The honored British author and journalist Malcolm Muggeridge made the phrase "the Great Liberal Death Wish" famous in an address to students and faculty at Hillsdale College in Michigan in 1979. Muggeridge, a leftist in his youth, had turned against socialism and Communism in the 1930s, ahead of other Western intellectuals, thus anticipating the conversion of George Orwell to a similar viewpoint by several years.

Muggeridge was moved in his Hillsdale speech by his aversion to abortion-on-demand, but his "liberal death wish" understanding was a wider one, encompassing what he had earlier perceived to be a politically correct blindness by his own colleagues to the crimes of the Soviet state. From this strange blindness to the cruelty of the Stalinist system by members of the Western intelligentsia, Muggeridge developed what he described as "my sense that Western man was, as it were, sleep-walking into his own ruin." He remarked on how "astonishingly deluded" the intellectual elite of Western countries were, blinded by their own idealism.

There is an eerie similarity between his time and ours and this study serves as a wake-up call to the sleepwalkers in the establishment and among the general public regarding a cluster of unresolved threats and crises, some of which have festered for decades. The book also provides positive suggestions for solutions and renewal, based on existing political institutions. The failure of liberal Democrats and "country club" Republicans to deal with challenges has inspired the "tea party" movement, a grassroots political revolt that has already toppled some long-time incumbents and helped engineer some astonishing election victories, including the loss of Ted Kennedy's Massachusetts U.S. Senate seat to a Republican, Scott Brown, and a historic shift in the House of Representatives in the 2010 Congressional elections, with Republicans picking up 63 seats, changing a 255-179 Democrat majority to a 242-193 Republican majority. As with the Ross Perot reform movement of 1991-96, this grassroots movement is likely to last for several years. In large majorities, polls show the general public exasperated with establishment policies on immigration, federal court activism, response to Iran's nuclear weapons program, federal spending, Obamacare and other issues. There is a disconnect between the American public and the American political class – and much is at stake.

Today the United States has begun to resemble pre-war Britain and France in terms of indifference to challenges. It is almost as if a death wish were now operating within the American elite, as it did among Western European elites in the 1930s. If the "great liberal death wish" of Muggeridge is construed as "a great American death wish," it would explain much of what has happened in the U.S. over the past several decades in four problem areas:

- A leadership crisis has resulted from an increasingly bizarre system of choosing presidential candidates in what amounts to an *American Idol* exercise – the merging of entertainment with politics as the TV-dominated primaries supersede party conventions as the means of selecting nominees. The participants in the TV primary debates are for the most part self-nominated and rarely have the credentials for the important job they seek. As a result, novelty trumps experience and how a candidate looks and sounds on television has become more important to voters than qualifying work experience.

- A strange indifference to a massive invasion of the United States from Mexico and Central America. This invasion, which has been going on for decades, is having profound effects on the character of the historic American nation in terms of language, culture, poverty, crime, public expenses, and, most alarmingly, in the survival of the two-party political system.

- A disturbing usurpation of legislative authority by unelected judges – especially at the federal level. In recent decades the nomination of persons to the federal bench, especially to the Supreme Court, has been thoroughly politicized, with liberal presidents trying to pack the courts with left-libertarian activists and conservative presidents attempting to build majorities that favor "original intent" or "originalism" or some other interpretation that falls short of endorsing a free-wheeling activism. Activist interpretations can and do amount to a legislating from the bench that is blatantly political, but which carries the full force of the Constitution rather than the more flexible force of Congressional law. Such activism is a perversion of the intent of the Founders and has been accurately described as judicial dictatorship. That the Supreme Court numbers only nine persons, and that they are appointed for life and are never answerable to the voters, makes their rise to political power all the more pernicious. Democracy itself, as universally understood, can be negated entirely by judicial activism. The Ninth and Tenth Amendments make it clear that the Founders expected the Constitution to be limited and for most American activities to take place outside its authority.

* An equally strange indifference to the rise of a new axis of dictators (including a Marxist one on our doorstep in Venezuela) and the proliferation of nuclear weapons to these dictators, concomitant with a failure to develop proper missile defenses.

Over the past four decades or so, each of these four challenges has slowly developed into crisis mode. Yet three presidents in a row and all the Congresses during this period have refused to deal with these problems. Healthy societies meet challenges with intelligence, flexibility, inventiveness and resolve. These characteristics have been entirely absent from most presidents since the 1960s, with Ronald Reagan being the sole and welcome exception.

The odd and strongly libertarian and libertine impulses of the 1970s may well have distracted the public, perhaps permanently, from focusing its attention on dangers, threats and growing crises at home and abroad. That is a sociological premise and an elusive one, but what can be said with confidence is that political leaders in both parties have not responded effectively to these challenges and the Democratic party since the 1970s has deliberately exacerbated these problems by its movement toward socialism, isolationism and libertinism – which, taken together, amount to a kind of decadence that Muggeridge would have recognized.

The Anglo-American development of constitutional government, the rule of law, and the development of mass-based democracy (a process that began about 1688) is only the second wave of democratic government on a large scale in the history of the world. The first wave, from the fifth to first centuries BC, in Italy and Greece, was snuffed out by war, conquest and military dictatorship. There is no guarantee that this second wave will survive, despite its spread to countries as different as Sweden and India. If democracy disappears in the United States, either because of military attack or inward collapse of institutions, it is not likely to survive for long in many other places, given the appetite for power among dictators – who would seize the occasion of America's collapse to increase their own domains.

The survival of majority-rule democracy is at stake – and "majority rule" is the essence of democracy. Since 1688, more and more countries: Britain, the United States, then other English-speaking countries, and now many other nations, including Germany, Japan, Indonesia and India, have extended the voting franchise to their entire adult populations. From a narrow base of voters in the 18th and 19th centuries, majority rule democracy has become nearly universal in the most advanced nations of the world. Yet elites today, like those in centuries past, seek control through minority rule. Democracy has been compromised by government bureaucracies, aggressive courts, influential business corporations, "human rights" commissions, partisan unions and other special interest groups. Human rights commissions in the European Union, Canada and in some

American states are notorious for overriding democratically elected legislatures in a mirror image of power-hungry courts in the United States, Israel and other democracies. Many in the political and cultural establishments of the West today are distrustful of democracy and favor rule by minority elites of which they are members. There is little doubt that liberals in the United States would prefer one-party control – and that is something that can be achieved through mass immigration and an endless expansion of judicial power via the elaboration of the "evolving constitution" idea.

In general, on most issues, the American public shows better judgment, as expressed in polls and surveys, than the elites. It exhibits more common sense and a healthier survival instinct than Congressional, judicial and intellectual elites – or most recent presidents. The celebrated Yale historian, Samuel Huntington, author of *The Clash of Civilizations and the Remaking of World Order*, wrote that American and European elites were increasingly global in outlook, disdaining nationalism and posing as world citizens rather than as citizens of their own countries. Loyalty to country is replaced by loyalty to internationalism, to international business structures and to international political institutions. On issue after issue, the American people in the majority think one way, and the political elite in the opposite. Barack Obama is clearly one of these new world citizens. Polls and surveys showed him out of favor with the majority of Americans scarcely a year into his term of office – which didn't seem to bother him at all.

One of the strangest aspects of our predicament is the substitution of environmental concern, almost at the level of a religion, for practical efforts to prevent disaster in the areas just described. These crises are ignored in favor of an environmental crusade that transcends all other concerns as far as the establishment (and especially the Obama administration) is concerned. The efforts that should be applied to addressing these crises are instead channeled into a Quixotic effort to stop global warming and save every species (an impossibility). Environmentalists seem to want to freeze-frame the environment as it now exists, unmindful that Nature had already killed off about 98 per cent of all species of animals, birds, plants, fish and other creatures long before the advent of man. An asteroid hitting the planet and wiping out most life here is a perfectly natural event from the point of view of Mother Nature, but not to the environmentalists who romanticize her. Not that climate concerns are not an issue – but nuclear war, resulting in a planet-wide "nuclear winter," is a far more serious and imminent threat to the planet and its people than global warming and would kill enormously larger numbers of human beings.

Elites are strongly motivated by philanthropy and permissiveness (reflecting their own privileged status). This philanthropy/permissiveness outlook is widespread among cultural elites in both Europe and America, as is a utopian idealism about a new America or a new world. The idealists apparently want traditional America to die so that something better can be built in its place. Much that is successful in America must be torn down along with those who made things successful – hence capitalism must be replaced by socialism; the Anglo majority by a new minority majority; Judeo-Christianity must be overthrown by secularism;

democracy replaced by a one-party state; freedom of speech and expression smothered by government controls on radio and the Internet; American uniqueness and exceptionalism rejected in favor of global and one-world loyalties; economic growth hindered by regulation and taxation; individual and family responsibility replaced by a nanny state.

An aspect of this psychology seems to be moral superiority. A great show of guilt and political correctness (such as we see in Barack Obama's diplomacy) is a way of announcing how morally superior one is to those who celebrate America's wealth and power, as high school history books once did. The morally superior *anti-American* American is in league with all the underdogs of the world: the oppressed, the poor, illegal immigrants, those who don't or can't enjoy an American standard of living. Identifying with them instead of with the majority of Americans is a way for members of the elite to exercise spiritual philanthropy (while retaining their own wealth and privileges, of course).

The government, foundation, and liberal academic elites are also motivated by guilt, which they transfer from themselves to America at large. Their relationship to most Americans, in terms of wealth and influence, is similar to America's relationship to the other 200-odd countries of the world. The traditional view of America as an unparalleled success is embarrassing to liberal elitists, hence the rewriting of textbooks to emphasize much that is negative in U.S. history and to downplay the obvious successes. That America is the most prosperous, egalitarian, democratic, medically advanced and militarily strongest country in world history – and that this was accomplished for the most part by ordinary people (as Eric Hoffer pointed out in numerous books) is largely ignored.

That members of the liberal elite in America subscribe to an ideological, anti-majority premise is obvious in the many occasions in which students have been punished for having Bibles in classrooms or on school buses, reprimanded for choosing Jesus as their favorite hero in a class assignment, rebuked for drawing an American flag or wearing a T-shirt with the flag on it, or, in one instance, praying silently outside the Supreme Court building. As Michael Reagan has often said, what used to be sacred is now profane and what used to be illegal or repugnant is now sacred (pornography, abortion). Many new history textbooks decry American achievements and indoctrinate children in a dreary anti-Americanism.

The elitist outlook is a strange combination of moral superiority, philanthropy and permissiveness, guilt, snobbery, and political correctness. This orientation supports left-libertarian political causes, including the unlimited growth of central government. The new intellectual class, which has vastly expanded since the 1960s, is made up of teachers and professors, most of them employed by government, college-educated press and media people who attended the elite (mostly East Coast) universities, and government, foundation, and university bureaucrats. The foot soldiers for the movement are labor union members, government employees, and minority voters dependent on government. Immigration aimed at adding as many disadvantaged people as possible to our population in the shortest period of time is another factor buoying up the elite and its church, the Democratic Party. Political correctness is a social bond for these people, even for those with a parvenu background. Members of this New Class, to borrow a term from the ex-Communist Milovan Djilas (his rueful term for the Communist autocracy that betrayed the people's revolution), are united in their disdain for majority rule – until, of course, they engineer a new majority. This New Elite meets Muggeridge's definition of the intelligentsia of his day as being naïve and credulous. The New Class subscribes fully to the philanthropy/permissiveness code: philanthropy for everyone via unlimited expansion of the central government, regardless of cost; permissiveness, of the show business variety, for all, thus rescuing the individual from the traditional constraints of the larger community and its religion. This model perfectly fits show business liberals as philanthropy is an avocation with them, just as permissiveness is their lifestyle. What characterized Hollywood for so long must now characterize Peoria, too. Individual "rights" demand it. Thus the New Class endorses a weird combination of slavery and freedom – slavery to central government (of which Congress is the enforcing arm), combined with libertine permissiveness (with the courts the enforcing arm).

The New Class has little or no sense of the consequences of these policies in a competitive world. Fiscal bankruptcy from spiraling government debt and the collapse of the dollar will lead to disaster for America, as will an isolationism that allows every dictator to acquire nuclear weapons.

Finally, one thread that runs through all of the obvious failures to meet challenges is the weakness of the American Congress. The American Constitution established Congress as the strongest of the three branches of government and the federal judiciary as the weakest (contrary to the error, widely cited, that the branches are co-equal). Instead of the intended hierarchy, Congress-President-Courts, the reality of today is Courts-President-Congress. Congress is lagging because it has relinquished much of its constitutional authority to presidents and courts. Most seriously, it has relinquished legislative authority to the courts, whose judges have eagerly accepted their new responsibilities, making the Supreme Court a super legislature, beyond the voters and beyond the purview of Congress. In Britain, courts do not overthrow laws of Parliament and even in Canada, where they occasionally do, Parliament has a check and balance and can overturn a court's ruling. In America, there is no check or balance on courts when judicial review is exercised by them, despite a total absence of judicial review in the Constitution.

The purpose of *The Great Liberal Death Wish* is to expose the irrationality of establishment behavior in the face of today's multiple life-or-death challenges. It defines the death wish mentality, which is fueled by guilt and political correctness. An alternative ideology based on the optimism of the Enlightenment as expressed in traditional British, American and European political culture, is offered as a basis for change and improvement. A pragmatic return to a limited American Constitution, with its obvious marriage of Calvinism and the Enlightenment, offers a practical approach to critical problems. A renewed sense of citizenship, a military stronger and more sophisticated than those of the dictators, a healthy federal system, a free enterprise economy and health care system, a vibrant and inclusive two-party political system, majority rule, and a limited judiciary are preferred to isolationism, judicial tyranny, minority rule, censorship of political debate, and socialism.

This book is in two parts: Decline and Renewal, and Anglo-American Civilization. The first and much larger section, on "decline," enumerates four problem areas and suggests remedies within our constitutional, federal system. The Anglo-American section reaffirms the basic Anglo-American principles developed from the Glorious Revolution of 1688-89 in Britain to the development of democracy in the United States and elsewhere in later centuries.

PROLOGUE

As Arnold Toynbee and others have pointed out, civilizations must successfully meet challenges – or they die. Anglo-American civilization has met life-or-death challenges in three world wars: World War I, World War II, and the Cold War, 1945-91. On June 6, 1944, there were perhaps ten viable democracies in the world. Two were Switzerland and Sweden, neutral in the war. Six of the others were English-speaking countries, of which five were at war with Hitler and Japan. On June 6, 1944, largely English-speaking armies – from Canada, America and Britain – landed on the shores of France and began an 11-month military campaign that proved to be as momentous as any military operation in centuries. Successfully waged, it defeated Hitler in the West while simultaneously saving Western Europe from Stalin and Soviet Communism. More than that, it planted a time-bomb that would go off almost half a century later and bring down Communism in Eastern Europe. Because West Germany and Western Europe were free and prosperous, Eastern European totalitarianism was gradually undermined, as termites undermine a building. Hallowed out and weak, the rotten structure of Communism in Eastern Europe collapsed in 1989 and then, to the amazement of the world, collapsed in Russia itself in 1991. The people of Russia and Eastern Europe knew that Western citizens were free and prosperous – and that they were not. That knowledge so undermined the authority of the social-fascist regimes in Eastern Europe that, when stressed, they collapsed almost overnight.

The West was blessed with exceptional leaders during and just after World War II: Winston Churchill, Franklin Roosevelt, Charles De Gaulle, Konrad Adenauer, Harry Truman. During the 1980s, as Communism began to collapse, another extraordinary generation of leaders emerged to oppose Soviet Russia, which had just completed a massive buildup of nuclear arms. These leaders were Pope John Paul II, Margaret Thatcher, Ronald Reagan, Helmut Kohl and Francois Mitterrand. Like their counterparts four decades earlier, they met the great challenge of their day and triumphed.

The contrast between these leaders and those we have suffered under since the '90s is dramatic. It is almost impossible to imagine a weaker or more corrupt French leader than Jacques Chirac, president from 1995 to 2007, or a weaker or more corrupt German leader than Gerhard Schroder, chancellor from 1998-2005 (fittingly, they were close friends). Italy's disgraced Silvio Berlusconi was not far behind them in infamy. Overlapping Chirac and Schroder were American presidents of unprecedented weakness, indecision and poor judgment – Bill Clinton and George W. Bush. Clinton also had the distinction of being as corrupt as Chirac, and like Richard Nixon, was one of the few presidents to commit a felony while in office.

As new life-or-death challenges faced the democracies, we

in the U.S. have had three weak presidents in a row. Clinton, George W. Bush, and, to date, Barack Obama – presidents unable to do anything sensible about myriad problems. Indeed, Clinton, Bush and Obama are all products of the foolish primary system, as was Jimmy Carter, another failed president.

In 1994, American voters turned out a Democratic Congress in record fashion, tossing out 54 Democrats in the House and delivering both houses of Congress to the Republicans for only the third time since 1928. Republicans dominated Congress for the next twelve years, during six of which they also held the presidency. What was the result? Every major problem continued to fester: the border remained wide open and the number of illegal aliens in America vastly increased; North Korea and Iran went forward, unhindered, with their nuclear weapons programs; federal judges continued their high-handed ways, often in violation of the Constitution; and neither party did anything about the shallow, TV-dominated method of selecting presidential nominees.

When Democrats took control of Congress in 2006 and of Congress and the presidency in 2008, they accelerated all the worst trends. Far from doing anything to meet the nation's challenges, the Democrats made the situation worse through massive spending of the pork barrel variety, a policy of placing liberal activists on the Court, and an apologetic foreign policy. The Democrats oppose any real border discipline and are eager to enroll illegal aliens *en masse* as voters, in what would amount to a political *coup* that would keep them comfortably in power for a century or longer. As a result of these and other policies, including a coercive national health care scheme, Democrats were punished in the 2010 congressional elections, losing some 63 House seats in one of the worst political setbacks in modern American history. But the U.S. Senate and the presidency remained Democrat, thus creating gridlock.

America is in a leadership crisis, one that has been developing since Ronald Reagan left office in January, 1989. Three weak presidents in a row have brought us to the brink. The American people are responding, in the Tea Party movement and in other ways, but many of the politicians are not stirring, despite that some of them who have contributed to the mess are now being defeated at the polls. An American majority in polls regularly disapproves of Barack Obama's presidency, a large majority feel the nation is on the wrong track, and an overwhelming majority disapproves of Congress.

New leadership will have to come from others, men and women like those who guided us through the Great Depression, the world wars and the Cold War. Whence will such leadership come? It may have to come from the middle classes, who generally do not subscribe to a death wish outlook and who maintain faith in a traditional America.

The bitter contempt the elites hold for the middle class is evident in their hatred of Sarah Palin, who is not only middle class, but blue collar middle class. What right does she have to challenge the political and cultural elites – the people who know better? She is not Ivy League, she does not have the smooth verbal delivery of the TV anchors, and she has the wrong cultural and social attitudes (anti-abortion, pro-gun). Smarmy comedians can't leave her alone, their late-night barbs dripping with venom – she is from the sticks, while they are in New York and Los Angeles. Yet she is emblematic of a growing middle class revolt against Barack Obama, Harry Reid, Nancy Pelosi, the various Bushes, and the Senate oligarchs of the political establishment.

The Tea Party movement, like the Perot reform movement of the early 1990s, is a manifestation of middle class impatience with the behavior of entrenched elites and incumbent politicians. Sarah Palin may never be a presidential candidate but she is a good spokesperson for the Tea Party movement. In fact, citizens are in the streets from both the left and right of the political spectrum, decrying elites in business and government that have lost touch with the people.

The most ominous threat to our survival comes from the new axis of dictators, some of them now acquiring nuclear weapons. These dictators are in close cooperation with one another – and Russia, a quasi-dictatorship under Vladimir Putin, is a main support of the new Axis. Russia has directly contributed to Iran's nuclear buildup and is moving to help Syria and Venezuela in the same fashion – supplying materials for nuclear power plants that will lead eventually to the refinement of materials for nuclear weapons. Politicians in the West have stood by in paralysis while these developments, which threaten the planet, human life on the planet, and democratic civilization, have accelerated. The world economy is also at risk, which makes inexplicable China's cowardice in response to these developments. But then, China itself is a dictatorship.

If any of the four crises are directly life-or-death issues, it is the new Axis and the proliferation of nuclear weapons. David

Frum, a speechwriter for President George W. Bush, coined the phrase, "axis of evil," which was then used by Bush several times to refer to North Korea, Iraq and Iran. The axis today would be North Korea, Iran and Venezuela, but Syria and others are waiting in the wings.

Allowing small dictatorships to develop nuclear weapons is the single most irrational decision made by American presidents in the two centuries the nation has existed. Three presidents in a row have been unable to deal with the challenge – which is why they are, alone or together, among the worst presidents in American history.

PART 1

DECLINE AND RENEWAL

THE FIRST CHALLENGE: LEADERSHIP

HOW POLITICS BECAME ENTERTAINMENT AND WHAT CAN BE DONE ABOUT IT

W eak presidents have paralleled Congressional weakness in the inept handling of the crises detailed in this book. After an impressive mid-century list of strong presidents (FDR, Truman, Eisenhower), we began a slide downward. How did this happen?

The presidential primaries were not decisive in the selection of presidential nominees until 1960, just in time for John F. Kennedy, the first show biz style presidential nominee. Many think Kennedy, with his charm and good looks, was responsible for the change, but the arrival of big time television news at about the same time had set the stage for Kennedy. Network television news had not been an especially important feature of the new medium, which had passed radio in popularity in most homes by about 1950. For some time network news was seen for only 5 minutes at 8 p.m., Eastern time, but in the summer of 1956 Chet Huntley and David Brinkley hosted the NBC-TV national political conventions and became overnight celebrities. Brinkley's dry wit and acerbic delivery made a nice contrast with Huntley's more sober demeanor. The two were rewarded with the first twin anchor of a network news broadcast, 15 minutes long, in the presidential election season that year – October, 1956. Eventually, they pulled ahead of the CBS 15-minute show opposite them in the same time slot.

Something was stirring in America at the time – a growing interest in political events and a growing appetite for news in general. This interest was a serious one and the presentation, especially a few years later by Walter Cronkite and others on CBS, had a compellingly serious tone (some said the tone was downright portentous). What was happening was that a growing segment of the media and entertainment market devoted to news (dramatically pronounced by some announcers as "neeuuws") was catching on with the American public. News being a commercial venture, then as now, the phenomenon would not have succeeded without a growing audience. Despite the fact that an entertainer such as Elvis Presley could be big news, the new medium was primarily devoted to politics and international events. The Cold War was at its most intense in the years 1956-63, with the Hungarian uprising, the Suez War (with its attendant nuclear missile threats from the Soviets), the Khrushchev-ruined summit meeting of 1960, a Berlin Crisis (twice), an ongoing Cuban imbroglio that culminated dramatically in the Cuban Missile Crisis of October, 1962 (in which nuclear war was narrowly averted), the turmoil of the civil rights struggles in the United States, and, finally, the biggest TV show of all, the murder and funeral of John F. Kennedy and the sideshow murder of his likely assassin, Lee Harvey Oswald, two days later. From Friday, November 22, 1963, through Monday, November 25, Americans paused to watch TV together in a communal drama melding shock with mourning.

This unprecedented era of TV news/entertainment would continue for more than a decade, encompassing both the Vietnam War and the Watergate events, before ebbing somewhat in public interest. During this period, roughly 1956 to 1976, the three major networks had a news monopoly for viewers of their now-expanded half hour dinner-time shows (CBS and NBC expanded to half an hour within weeks of each other in September-October, 1963, and the "news hour" shows went to color TV in the mid-sixties).

It was against this background that John F. Kennedy, the first TV president, ran for his abbreviated term in the White House. Dwight Eisenhower was the first president fully covered by TV, but he was not the first TV president. Harry Truman, generally regarded by historians as a "top ten" president, was a miserable performer on TV and could not be elected president today. He was a small, middle-aged man with a Missouri twang, little charisma and limited public speaking ability. That he followed a master manipulator of the media of his day, Franklin Roosevelt, didn't help. But Roosevelt, with his slow, stentorian drawl, would probably not have been a good candidate for TV, as Hubert Humphrey, a superb outdoor (think state fair) orator, was not. TV called for a cooler, quieter presentation, as many stage actors learned from their directors when they ventured into Playhouse 90 and Hallmark Hall of Fame live TV dramas in the 1950s and '60s. Kennedy, who did not have a good voice for outdoor or big venue speaking (his voice when pushed was hoarse and strained) was perfect for the more intimate medium of television, especially television news conferences, where he could use his ready wit to parry the over-earnest questioning of TV reporters who didn't seem to mind his ability to get a public laugh at their expense and responded by treating him with a respect he wanted the nation to witness. Kennedy was good-looking (and younger looking than his age), exceptionally bright, and verbally gifted. His only job, other than politics and military service, had been journalism, and he often spoke of becoming a newspaper publisher after his White House years, so as to remain an observer and commentator on the passing political scene. With his youth, glamour and engaging wit, he made a stark contrast with President Eisenhower's tangled syntax, premature aging, and halting verbal manner (though Ike's famous grin looked as good on television as on a *Saturday Evening Post* cover). Interestingly, this was the beginning of a misjudgment of politicians by the American public, who over-appreciated Kennedy – for the wrong reasons – and under-appreciated Ike – again, for the wrong reasons. Eisenhower's lack of glibness did not interfere with his administrative and decision-making abilities, his judgment of character in others, or his sense of balance in international and domestic political policy. Eisenhower, who was never popular with the intelligentsia (they favored the "egghead" Adlai Stevenson), was dumped by historians into the bottom ten of a survey of American presidents taken in 1962 (one of the periodic surveys by historians and political scientists overseen by the late Arthur Schlesinger, Jr.). Miraculously, when a survey was done again in the early '80s, Eisenhower had leaped from political hell to heaven, landing in the top ten, largely because he had avoided the temptation to join in the Vietnam War while JFK and Lyndon Johnson had not. That, plus a one-man rehabilitation campaign by maverick historian and best-selling author, Stephen Ambrose, has regularly placed Eisenhower above Kennedy in such surveys. The public, taken in by JFK's media performance, mistakenly felt he was the better man, and would make a better president. They were wrong then and have been wrong ever since. Even today, Kennedy is routinely rated in public surveys as one of America's best presidents. In truth, John F. Kennedy was much too young and inexperienced to be elected president at a critical juncture in the Cold War. He would have been an attractive candidate for vice-president, having served 14 years in the House and Senate (though ill and absent from the floor long stretches of that time). It may be true that Kennedy was emerging as a world statesman in his third year in office, but just before his own death he accepted the overthrow of the president of South Vietnam and his family and seemed bent on pursuing the war there (an attitude echoed by his advisors, inherited by Lyndon Johnson, who remained stubbornly hawkish all the way into the disaster years of 1967-68). Kennedy's deteriorating health – a back problem may have put him in a wheel chair during a second term – and his reckless womanizing, might also have derailed his presidency, had he survived Dallas.

Kennedy became president by using the primary system, a system joined at the hip with television. Primaries had existed before Kennedy's run in 1960, but they had not been especially important (the first primaries were established in places like

Oregon – 1910 – where Progressive era reforms were taken up with enthusiasm, the idea being to make the process more democratic and less a matter for machine politicians in back rooms). But only a handful of states had primaries until much later, and the primaries were not decisive. For example, Tom Dewey had done very well in the 1940 Republican primaries, but faded at the convention, where – after six ballots – he lost to a newcomer, Wendell Willkie. A similar scenario unfolded in 1944, when Harold Stassen did surprisingly well in the primaries, but lost to Dewey at the Republican convention.

The 1952 and 1956 conventions were decisive in the nominations for both parties and were covered by the networks gavel to gavel, from early morning until late at night. John Kennedy had a big TV moment when he almost unseated Estes Kefauver as Adlai Stevenson's running mate at the 1956 convention, then graciously asked the delegates to endorse Kefauver with a voice vote. This brief but impressive audio-visual moment got people talking about Kennedy as a possible nominee in the future, much as Ronald Reagan's appearance in 1964, in favor of Barry Goldwater's nomination, provided a favorable image Reagan could cultivate 12 years later with his own presidential run.

Kennedy blitzed the 1960 primaries with money, an army of volunteers that included most of his glamorous relatives, tireless energy, and a sure sense of what worked on television. His most serious primary opponent was the ebullient Hubert Humphrey of Minnesota, champion of minorities, union members and the poor, who was stunned when defeated in Wisconsin, his neighboring state, by the Kennedy machine. When he also lost West Virginia he realized the game was up.

Kennedy's most serious convention opponent was the wily Lyndon Johnson, the experienced Senate Majority Leader – an arm bender and enforcer who knew where all the bodies were buried and who could call on all who owed him favors. As *Time* magazine put it, in a witty cover article a few weeks before the election, he fell short by a nose. Kennedy's looks, charisma, TV savvy and a finely tuned organization led by his devoted brother, Bobby, were too much for Johnson, who ended up second on the ticket, a move that won Texas' electoral votes and the election – by the slightest of margins. America and the world would have been better off if the ticket had been LBJ/JFK instead of the reverse (and might have been if the convention activities had trumped the primaries as they had before 1960).

Kennedy's inexperience and the know-it-all idealism of his young Ivy League advisors and cabinet members, combined with JFK's rush to do too much too soon, led to a series of unfortunate foreign policy directives in the early weeks of the presidency of America's youngest elected president: a premature and ill-advised summit meeting with the brutish Nikita Khrushchev that led to many disasters, including a Berlin crisis and Khrushchev's decision to put nuclear missiles into Cuba in 1962 (because Kennedy expressed such fear of nuclear weapons when they met), plus the Bay of Pigs invasion of Cuba, which convinced Castro he needed the missiles – and, just three weeks into his presidency (according to a friendly biographer, Richard Reeves), a decision to draw a line in the sand against "Communism" in Vietnam, because he could do nothing about Cuba, Berlin or Laos. The Vietnam War, which went on for 12 years and ruined two American presidents, was one of the premier follies in the history of the American presidency – and it took the lives of some three million people. LBJ would have had a different cabinet – with more Texans and more old pros and fewer young, hard-edged idealists.

Kennedy did not win the nomination in the primaries, but the primaries provided the momentum he needed to win on an early ballot at the convention. Rarely would a convention be that close again – the 1968 Democratic and 1976 Republican conventions being exceptions that proved the rule, for in both cases winners in primaries almost overcame incumbent, convention favorites.

The arrival of Kennedy and the promotion of television as a decisive influence on choosing future presidents were not lost on Norman Mailer, a keen student of the passing political scene and much more. Mailer's colorful study of JFK's win at the 1960 convention was published as an article in *Esquire* magazine, "Superman Comes to the Supermarket," November, 1960, considered today one of the seven best articles ever to appear in *Esquire*. Mailer understood that JFK's charm was an avenue to power, that his image was more important than substance, that novelty bested experience in the new political game.

Mailer wrote of "the winds of High Television," and of a Kennedy who was "unlike any politician who had ever run for president." He described Los Angeles as a kind of bland supermarket where anything could be packaged in plastic for mass consumption. The Democrats, by design, he wrote, were about to nominate "a great box office actor, and the consequences of that were staggering." In the city famous for

Hollywood, the Democrats were choosing a candidate who would reach into "the dream life of the nation," a candidate for "mass man." Politics, with JFK, was becoming "America's favorite movie, America's first soap opera, America's best-seller." JFK "was like an actor who had been cast as the candidate."

This introduction to the supremacy of image over substance would become a standard feature of the primary system for nominating presidential candidates. JFK's run for president also introduced the baleful institution of TV "debates," which later degenerated, during the party primaries, into cattle shows in which a host of candidates (all self-nominated) on stage together, were gradually winnowed down in numbers as the weeks went by until only two were left as serious contenders. Unlike the hours-long Lincoln-Douglas debates, these debates – beginning with Kennedy-Nixon – were relatively brief, with candidates given 90 seconds to answer questions of mind-boggling complexity.

A survey of people who heard the first Kennedy-Nixon debate on radio, but did not see it on television, concluded that Nixon had won. The TV results were the opposite – the cool, handsome, articulate Kennedy seemed a clear winner in that crucial first debate (others followed) over the sweating Nixon, with his five o' clock shadow prominent on black and white TV, and his answers ground out in his deep, dark voice. Up to that time, Nixon had been a few points ahead of Kennedy in the Gallup and other polls; afterward, the two were more or less even, down to the last weekend of the campaign. JFK's TV performance, which included a preposterous pledge to defend two rocky little islands (Quemoy and Matsu) much closer to mainland China than to Taiwan, probably won him the presidency in one of the closest elections in presidential election history (given the irregularities in voting in Illinois and Texas, and the strange manner in which delegates were chosen in Alabama, it is likely Nixon had a plurality of the vote, if it could ever be accurately and honestly counted). But Kennedy would be president, the first of many not ready for the rigors of the office, but winners in the image department.

Television, in both the primaries and the general election campaigns, came to dominate presidential politics. This was in stark contrast to the British system, in which television traditionally played a minor role and in which, because of the parliamentary system, the prime minister had to be a man or woman of substantial experience and leadership. Televised debates in Britain for the first time in 2010 did have an impact – an unfortunate one, as the third party candidate, Nick Clegg, because of his impressive "performance" on the "telly," hurt the Conservative candidate, David Cameron, enough to force a coalition government. Without the debates, Cameron would likely have won a clear majority and organized a new Conservative-dominated government. Clegg, a man of little substance (more socialist spending at home and "a world without nuclear weapons" abroad), was a good TV performer, a good actor. In fairness, in terms of being a good TV performer, the same could be said of Tony Blair, elected Prime Minister three times. But TV or no TV, all nominees in the U.K. were veteran parliamentarians, in contrast to the amateurs arising in the American system – Barack Obama being the most glaring example.

In the British system only the leaders of the three parties in

Parliament, three persons only, can become Prime Minister. No businessman, military leader, public administrator, mayor, political gadfly, or private citizen, however remarkable, has any chance of leading the nation – except by entering politics, getting elected to Parliament and then spending many years moving up the leadership ladder to become head of his or her respective party.

Despite the differences in the systems there has not been much diversity in the U.S., either. In the century or so from Theodore Roosevelt's presidency to Barack Obama's, about half of our presidents have been members of Congress and the other half former governors. Some were both, and only three (Taft, Hoover and Eisenhower) were neither. We have had good luck with governors of the most populous states at the time (Theodore Roosevelt, Franklin Roosevelt, and Ronald Reagan), but less agreeable service from some other governors (notably Jimmy Carter, Bill Clinton, and George W. Bush). Going to the British system would eliminate governors, unless they were smart enough to run for Congress after serving in state houses – which is likely.

The innovation of the TV-dominated process for selecting nominees, centered on the primaries, was always irresponsible. As primaries proliferated after 1960, many of them were open to cross-over voters. Seldom did the vote of registered party members in a Democratic or Republican primary rise much above 10 per cent of registered party voters in the state (the Clinton/Obama campaign of 2008 was a notable exception). Obviously, to serve party discipline to any meaningful degree, primaries should be closed to the opposite party but open to independents (so as to prevent ideological hardliners from dominating the nomination process). Caucuses are even worse as a measure of party loyalty. Normally, as anyone who has ever attended a caucus knows, a handful of people show up. During election years, enthusiasts for a candidate or a cause can flood a caucus and take the proceedings away from the usual party members and elect new precinct leaders, adopt new platforms, and endorse a candidate of the moment. The Reverend Pat Robertson's surprise second-place finish in the Iowa caucuses in 1988 was just such an exercise in minority activism, as was Pat Buchanan's surprise win in the New Hampshire primary of 1996. The similarly surprising second place finish of Minnesota Senator Eugene McCarthy in the 1968 New Hampshire primary is another example. Though the incumbent president, Lyndon Johnson, won the primary (and did it the hard way, with a write-in vote), the TV networks and pundits shouted that McCarthy had really won – and that result, in combination with polls showing him slipping in Wisconsin and other primaries, encouraged Johnson to withdraw from the race. The foolishness of having the earliest primary in a tiny state like New Hampshire as a beacon (along with the equally foolish habit of including Iowa's caucuses in the same role) has encouraged political mavericks to look to these two early season media events to hype their candidacies. Candidates who were clearly not the leaders of their respective parties – Barry Goldwater, JFK, George McGovern, Jimmy Carter, Bill Clinton, George W. Bush, Barack Obama – all have benefited from the primary system, in which television performance or novelty could be resourcefully used to create images of leadership that had little or no substance in reality. In general, Democrats have been more susceptible to the process than Republicans, whose voters often reward loyalty, as when the Republicans threw away two of the last four presidential nominations on dull men over 70, neither of whom had a prayer in the general election. Democrats have nominated the two most glamorous of the unprepared, JFK and Barack Obama – and Obama is very likely the least experienced president in American history.

The primaries favor candidates with movie star appeal, and Ronald Reagan was just that – a master of the teleprompter (as is Obama) and a man who knew instinctively how to build and maintain a public image and how to communicate to average Americans. When asked once if his training as a Hollywood actor helped him in the job, Reagan genially replied that it was indispensable. But "the great communicator" was a shrewd politician and a man of substance, intellectually. The publication after his death of Reagan's letters, notes and diaries reveals a man with a grasp of history, a detailed knowledge of foreign affairs, a keen sense of the need for compromise, and a depth that many did not appreciate at the time. Like Franklin Roosevelt, Reagan had to respond to not one, but two crises – in his case, the Cold War *and* a moribund economy. Because he responded with energy and intelligence to both challenges, while resurrecting a tarnished presidency and simultaneously abolishing a national malaise from the Vietnam-Watergate-Carter years, he is now rated highly by most historians and by the general public. He was the first two-term president and the first genuinely successful president since Eisenhower.

Reagan, however, had been a successful two-term

governor of our largest state, a former two-time president of a major union, and a longtime spokesman for free enterprise capitalism, crisscrossing the nation as a representative for General Electric. He was also one of the oldest presidents ever elected, turning 70 early in his first term. He may have been a media darling, but he was in many respects a seasoned, wise old man who knew just what he wanted to do as president. Reagan never had a Republican House of Representatives to work with and the Democrats controlled the Senate the last half of his second term, so he was obliged to exercise bipartisanship, which he did with aplomb. The contrast with JFK, Jimmy Carter, Bill Clinton and Barack Obama is instructive. None of them were ready for the presidency and three were in their forties.

Carter and Bush crafted folksy images of themselves – Carter as the man of the people who, as an outsider, would restore integrity and honesty in Washington. He capitalized on his lack of experience – he wasn't part of the problem. Ironically, because he had so little experience in Washington, he failed there. While he was an articulate TV performer, he had almost none of the gifts of leadership Reagan had in such abundance and the voting public rejected him after one term, as they did the aloof George H.W. Bush a few years later. George W. Bush, the latter's son, more awkward as a speaker but able to reasonably negotiate the debates with Vice President Al Gore and Senator John Kerry, used his ties to his father's administration to suggest he would bring a seasoned hand to foreign and domestic affairs.

Carter, who was blindsided by the Iranian Revolution and the Russian invasion of Afghanistan, lost touch with the American people, and was completely helpless in effecting the release of over 100 U.S. Embassy staff members held as captives for over a year in Iran in gross violation of international law.

Bill Clinton, the next media favorite to use the primaries for a premature rise to the presidency, was dogged endlessly by the scandals that preceded him in Arkansas – political, sexual, and financial. He lied his way out of most of these eruptions, but the two personal lawyers he brought with him to Washington paid a high price: one committed suicide and the other was sent to prison. Clinton's good looks, hurt lip look, and soft voice – and his extraordinary ability to spin versions of events in his favor, kept him going until an incredibly stupid sexual misadventure inspired him to perjury and the second impeachment of a president in American history.

Clinton wasted eight years trying to bribe North Korea to stop building nuclear weapons while the dictatorship there used the proceeds to build nuclear weapons. He sent his Secretary of State, Madeleine Albright, to North Korea for a farcical state visit that was typical of his sleight-of-hand politics – lots of show, little substance. The Iranian nuclear weapons project got a solid start under Clinton, too, and the open borders immigration disaster grew apace, despite a few positive steps in the San Diego area. Like George H.W. Bush before him, he also neglected missile defense programs. Despite some solid achievements (welfare reform among them) it is not unreasonable to include Clinton with James Buchanan, George W. Bush and Barack Obama as one of the four most ineffective presidents in our history. Clinton was very much a child of television, a clever performer, an actor pretending to be president. Like Kennedy, he would have profited from a term or two as vice president. Yet his post-presidential philanthropic efforts have been commendable and he remains popular with voters who remember his balanced budgets and the solid economic growth of his years in Washington.

Like Clinton, George W. Bush also allowed eight years to pass while doing nothing effective to stop the Iranian and North Korean nuclear weapons and missile programs. Worse, he squandered the nation's military capacities and the willingness of the American people to bear the burden of war with an unnecessary invasion of Iraq in 2003. When it was discovered after the overthrow of the Saddam Hussein regime that Iraq had few, if any, weapons of mass destruction, Bush and Vice President Cheney would have to have resigned had they been in the British system (Tony Blair eventually paid the price for his participation in this unnecessary war, stepping down a year and a half early from his third term in the United Kingdom). Bush also allowed the immigration disaster to get completely out of control, despite that the 9/11 terrorist attacks had provided a perfect excuse for closing the border.

Bush and Clinton benefited from the primary system and from TV advertising, the other side of the coin of politics as entertainment. TV ads work, as millionaire Michael Huffington, a neophyte with only two years experience in the House of Representatives, discovered when he ran against U.S. Senator Diane Feinstein in California in 1994. Spending heavily on TV advertising, he managed to pull ahead of the more experienced and better known Feinstein in the polls, forcing Feinstein and her wealthy husband to dig deeper into their own pockets to spend their way back to the lead, which they did.

The absurd TV ads touting inexperienced people like Barack Obama for the presidency on the basis of looks and public speaking ability, are now the rule rather than the exception. John Edwards was yet another example of the Hollywood style candidate, with little or no relevant experience, catapulted to a vice presidential nomination and later considered a viable presidential candidate by Democrats. The utter collapse of his career in a shambles of personal folly bears witness to his lack of character – which matched his lack of experience. But he looked *so good* on television. Most of the failed presidents were elected because TV ads fashioned images the public responded to favorably: Jimmy Carter, the latter day Mr. Smith heading to Washington; Clinton and Gore, a handsome pair of young reformers who felt our pain; JFK, accepting the torch of leadership for a new generation; Barack Obama, lifting his head and looking off to the invisible mountains on his right, where he no doubt could already see his visage carved in stone.

Yet as awful as these presidents have been, Bill Clinton might easily have been reelected to a third term, and possibly even a fourth. JFK was a shoo-in for a second term, and Obama may win a second term, despite his catastrophic Congressional losses in the 2010 mid-term elections. The lesson here is obvious: the 22nd Amendment is one of the sterling accomplishments of Congress in its entire history – because it limits presidents, including the worst ones, to two terms.

Barack Obama's election owed much to the ineptness of

George W. Bush, but his qualifications were largely created out of thin air – such things as dreams are made on. Sifting through the grab bag of short-term, part-time jobs Obama held before landing for a few years in the Illinois legislature, you find only one meaningful employment – a dozen years as a part-time lecturer in the University of Chicago law school. He had no viable other career job. Obama had almost no experience in the business world, no military service, no experience in the cabinet, no administrative experience, and only four years in the U.S. Senate – which he used as a platform to run for president, having geared up for the run his second year there. His record in the Senate was undistinguished and featured an unusual number of "present" votes, a habit he carried over from the Illinois legislature.

But Obama looks and sounds good on television, which is the main requirement these days. His naïve approach to Iran and North Korea, his total lack of bipartisanship, his wild rush to socialize the medical insurance system in America, his appetite for an ever-growing federal government with deficits to match, and his keen desire to enroll as many illegal aliens as possible as voters, all bode ill for our nation.

Obama is only the second president to come out of academia. The other academic was Woodrow Wilson, eventually destroyed by his own idealism and egocentricity. But Wilson had a good deal more practical experience than Obama. He was a full professor, for one thing, and served as president of Princeton University for eight years. This led to a run for the governorship of New Jersey, which he won, serving as a reform governor for two years before launching a presidential run in 1912. Wilson was a great, but flawed man, who lacked the street smarts to take on the wily and brutal politicians of Europe in the peace negotiations at the end of World War I. His dream (some would say fantasy) of a world at peace via a League of Nations, was pursued with such intensity – and such arrogance – that his health broke, his presidency collapsed, and his dream died with him. Yet, as noted, he was far more experienced than Obama, who shows similar tendencies toward naïve visions.

The entertainment that politics has become in the United States may well become a horror movie in not too many years, as damage is done by the poorly prepared and often flawed politicians who looked and sounded so good on television. This is in sharp contrast to the sober, solid performance in power of every British Prime Minister since Winston Churchill's first term.

A simple remedy for primary election reform would be to grant only half the state's delegates in its primary. The other half of the delegates would be chosen in the old-fashioned way, and many if not most would be uncommitted going into the conventions – and a real fight would ensue for the nomination at those conventions, which would be restored to their previous importance. This would bring many interests and factions into play at the same time in each primary. The front-loaded schedule of primaries we now have could be corrected by holding four "time zone" primaries, one each in February, March, April and May. These time zones would bring in many ethnic groups and geographic interests simultaneously and would not have the odd provincialism of the New Hampshire primary and of the Iowa caucuses. A plan along these lines was endorsed at a convening of the secretaries of state of the American state governments. Ideally, primaries would be open to independents but not to voters registered in the other party. This would keep Democrats from voting in Republican primaries and vice versa, but would leaven the party vote with independent voices, which might help pull each of the major parties back to the political center, which has been empty lately.

The rush in recent years to push all or most of the primaries to earlier dates makes for an even more superficial exercise, even more dependent on TV imaging. The best Republican candidate in 2008 was Mitt Romney, a centrist conservative with a solid background in the business world and impressive experience as an administrator of the 2002 Winter Olympics – having also been a popular governor of Massachusetts where he was able to successfully work with the Democratic majority in the state legislature. Instead of Romney as nominee the party got another Bob Dole figure in John McCain, clearly at a serious disadvantage in terms of age, enthusiasm, energy and charisma. McCain threw away his strongest feature, experience, by adding to his ticket a politician with almost as little experience as Barack Obama – Sarah Palin, who lacked the experience to be president if something happened to the elderly McCain. After the election, Palin, as an instant political/entertainment celebrity, promptly quit her job as governor and did the logical thing – hitting the lecture circuit and making as many TV appearances as possible while writing a best-selling book. All of this raked in millions of dollars for her and her family and she can't be blamed for that, but the downside is that all this TV hoopla is no substitute for administrative or Congressional experience.

Liberals, especially those who are professional intellectuals, are unanimous in defaming Palin's intelligence – largely on the basis of her vocabulary and syntax in the 2008 campaign and her relative naivete on foreign policy and some other issues. But anyone who has seen Palin on television a few years later can attest that her speaking vocabulary is as good as that of any professional talking head on network TV and that she has been a quick study on the issues.

Palin was ambushed by Katie Couric in the famous TV interview in which, when asked what news sources she consulted or read, she couldn't come up with a single title. Liberals read the newsmagazines *Time* and *Newsweek,* monthlies like *The Atlantic* and *Harpers,* weeklies like *The Nation* and the *New Republic,* dailies such as the *New York Times* and *Washington Post,* and online sources such as Moveon.org and the *Huffington Post.* It is quite possible that at the time Palin read none of these, which would make her an ignoramus in the eyes of the liberal intelligentsia. Judging from her nuanced remarks more recently, on economic and foreign policy issues, Palin is now reading some of those sources – and more. She has charisma to burn, good political instincts, intelligence, energy and enthusiasm, but she lacks the longtime knowledge, sobriety (or "gravitas" to employ an overused term) that you would look for in a chief executive who would have to wrestle with extremely complex military, economic and diplomatic problems and challenges. It takes years – if not decades – of work, study and practical experience to earn that kind of background. Politicians such as John Edwards, Barack Obama, Sarah Palin and, more recently, Herman Cain, have lacked that background.

Reforming the nominating system involves no constitutional issues, so the respective parties and the states are free to make changes for the good of the nation. The Democrats have made major changes in nominating rules since 1968, abolishing the winner-take-all awarding of delegates in primaries (thus depriving Mrs. Clinton of an easy nomination win in 2008). Unfortunately, the effort to be fair to every minority and small group, has all but killed majority rule in the Democratic Party and has allowed an inexperienced but careful student of the system, Barack Obama, to manipulate it into winning a nomination he didn't deserve and would likely never have received from the old-line and more professional Democratic nominating conventions of the past. Obama represented novelty and telegenic virtues, but little substance. Republicans have now duplicated some of this silliness by adopting share-voting in some of their primaries and pushing the Iowa caucus to the absurdly early date of January third.

Some would say that returning nominating authority to the conventions would restore the "smoke-filled room," approach to nomination, as party bosses huddle and make backroom deals of the sort that advanced the woeful Warren Harding to the Republican nomination in 1920. This may be true (keeping in mind that half the delegates would still be winnable for one or more ballots in the primaries) but a bit of behind the scenes political muscle by professionals would not be a bad thing, considering the amateur candidates and presidents we have suffered with.

It is unlikely that Democrats will do anything to reform the nominating system, but the Republicans had a golden opportunity going toward 2012. Sadly, the Republican Party, under such tepid leaders as Mitch McConnell, former Speaker of the House Denny Hastert, present Speaker John Boehner, and former RNC chairman Michael Steele, has shown little imagination and offers no representative Republican voice on this or many other issues. Innovation has not been a Republican strong suit.

Change in the nominating process is relatively easy compared to changes in the structure of the government itself. The British have an astonishingly democratic system in which a parliamentary majority can pass sweeping legislation by a simple majority vote – with no presidential veto and little or no interference from the courts. That may be too sweeping for a country like ours, with its regional differences and huge minority populations.

American presidents, products of the TV-influenced primary system, have been increasingly inept, unprepared and out of touch. More and more they are primarily ceremonial in much of what they do. Bill Clinton, indefatigable in promoting his own image, never stopped campaigning after he was elected in 1992, giving rise to the phrase, "the permanent campaign." Clinton acted as though he had been elected mayor of America, not president of America. He was forever elbowing into every photo op, including the one for the Mars Rock – a geological find which was supposed to prove that life originated on Mars. It didn't, but Clinton had his face in the photo just in case.

Of the three recent failed presidents, Clinton had the most to offer and accomplished the most. He came from a lower middle class background in Arkansas and graduated from

Yale Law School. He had intelligence, charm, political skills, communication skills, an intellect, and a strong measure of common sense. Politically he was more of a centrist than a leftist. He did better on North Korea and immigration than either of the Bushes or Obama, yet failed on both issues. When his wife's ambitious, government-dominated health care bill went down in flames in 1994, taking the Democrat majorities in both houses of Congress with it, Clinton was smart enough to pull a 180 degree political turn and declare that "the era of big government is over." Dealing with a Republican Congress for the six remaining years of his presidency, he avoided major policy pitfalls, supported a historic welfare overhaul, got family leave and some health insurance extensions for the middle class, balanced the budget and, to everyone's surprise – including his own – ran a few budget surpluses toward the end. Clinton rode the dotcom boom of the Nineties and wisely raised taxes only a bit (on the wealthiest) while avoiding new big government programs, thus keeping the economy growing so that government revenues rose in tandem with the economy to balance the federal budget. Compare that with the yearly *trillion* dollar deficits Obama has planned for years to come. Because of the economic good times and in spite of the Lewinsky mess and his impeachment by the House for perjury related to it, Clinton maintained the public's overall approval to the end and could probably have been elected to a third term, if one was available. Clinton had all the gifts and qualities to be a successful president, but he also had deep character flaws that kept him embroiled in political, personal and financial scandals. In the end, character did him in – and that was a shame.

George W. Bush was more of a failure than Clinton. He squandered his party's majority in Congress, allowed North Korea to build its bomb, invaded Iraq (thus doing nothing about Iran, the dictatorship that was *really* building nuclear weapons), and allowed the immigration disaster to become the crisis it is today by tolerating open borders for eight straight years. All of this combined to save the Democratic Party and propel it into power. Bush saw America not as a nation, but simply as an economy, hence his immigration ineptness. He apparently never understood that the McGovernized Democratic Party, falling off the cliff with its leftist politics, would be saved by Hispanic voters. Bush lost Congress in the middle of his second term and lost it again, by much wider margins, at the end of his presidency, thus paving the way for the disastrous Barack Obama, potentially the worst of the three failed presidents. Bush did achieve solid success with his projects to fight AIDS in Africa and elsewhere and to provide that continent with enhanced support. He convinced Congress to pass Medicare prescription coverage, a much-needed boon to middle class elderly, but he failed grievously on three of the four issues discussed in this book.

Americans would very likely prefer that their presidents be sitting in the oval office for a long day's work instead of hopping around the country to cut ribbons and do other mayoralty tasks that keep them before the TV cameras. The last three presidents have all been very good at the ceremonial (and largely meaningless) side of the presidency – and Obama, like Clinton, seems to relish this aspect of the job. Obama is devoting the second half of his term to campaigning for re-election, while providing little or nothing in the way of leadership or solid policy proposals to meet the crises of the day, including the government financial crisis. He is truly a do-nothing president.

How much better would it be if the executive branch of the government actually had a CEO – someone like Jack Welch, Bill Gates or Lee Iacocca – to supervise the federal government bureaucracy and make it work in the public interest, and within a reasonable budget? The gigantic debts we have been running under most presidents (with Obama the worst of all) are pulling America down to the level of Southern Europe in terms of fiscal health. California has already reached this point of financial collapse (representing, as it does, our great experiment in runaway welfare combined with runaway immigration). An interesting side note is that two successful businesswomen, Carly Fiorina, former CEO of Hewlett-Packard, and Meg Whitman, former CEO of eBay, entered the California political scene by running for U.S. Senate and governor, ostensibly to bring a more business-like style to government – but they were rejected by a tidal wave of Hispanic votes that maintained the corrupt and inept Democrat majorities in the state legislature, and promoted back to power a retread Democrat governor, Jerry Brown.

But could a CEO-style president also promote legislation, work with Congress, fulfill some of the ceremonial functions of the office, and serve as commander-in-chief of the armed forces? Probably not. A prime minister in Britain has these functions but he is embedded in parliament himself as a party leader and must depend heavily on his cabinet for the day-to-day running of the government. The British cabinet members have more authority and more to do than their American counterparts. All of them have ministerial rank, with their leader the "prime," or first, minister, as their boss.

This raises the interesting idea of somehow combining the British and American systems, which is what Charles De Gaulle did in 1958 in France, offering a hybrid model that has been copied by other countries, including Taiwan, Ukraine, and Egypt. Newt Gingrich would be an ideal prime minister, which he more or less was, briefly, in early 1995, when he addressed the nation over the head of President Clinton and made all the major news magazine covers after engineering a sweeping Republican victory in the House in November, 1994. Had he been prime minister in 1995-99, he would have put brakes on Clinton and might even have forced him to resign during the Lewinski scandal.

In a hybrid system the prime minister dominates and leads the legislative side of government while the president oversees foreign and military policy and the executive side of the government. The problem for us is that the British system is dominated by one legislative house, the House of Commons, which has the last word, while in ours the Senate and House of Representatives have equal status. It is difficult to see how an American prime minister (a glorified Speaker of the House) could control both House and Senate. Presumably, as in France, the president would still have a veto, anyway.

The job simply may be too much for one man and, perhaps, the vice-president could be given more to do, including some oversight of Congress to help advance the president's agenda there. Nevertheless, some way of merging a parliamentary system with a presidential one may be the most promising path to reform.

The distinguished political scientist and scholar James MacGregor Burns has spent his professional life wrestling with the problem of making the presidency work better, publishing his ideas in books that range from *The Deadlock of Democracy* (1963) to *Running Alone: Presidential Leadership from JFK to Bush II* (2006). It has been a major concern of his career and he has written at least half a dozen books on the subject. The separation of the executive from the legislative in the American system is a bugbear to him, but he stops short of endorsing a wholesale conversion to the parliamentary model. Basically, Burns is disappointed with all liberal presidents since Harry Truman, including even the one he personally campaigned for – John F. Kennedy. Holding a somewhat similar view is Daniel Lazare, whose fascinating study, *The Frozen Republic* (1996), deserved more attention than it got at the time of publication. Lazare argues that the Founding Fathers adopted a checks and balances system similar to the British traditional model, king-parliament-courts, just about the time (or a bit before) Britain began moving toward a parliament-first arrangement. It took Britain more than a century (until 1911) to get there, but that is essentially what they have now, while we are stuck with a frozen, deadlocked, balance-of-power arrangement in which presidential initiatives are blunted, Congress stews in its own rhetoric, and the courts run amok with power.

The American separation of the president from the legislature does have one significant virtue – it guarantees a two-party system. There is no advantage to coming in third, fourth or fifth in an American presidential election, whereas there is a very real advantage to do so in a parliamentary system, because holding even a few seats can make a small party a king-maker when a ruling coalition is being formed. It is the rule now that most parliamentary regimes have a difficult time winning solid majorities for one party. As in most European countries, and in Britain and Israel, various parties have to hammer out a working coalition, with even the smallest parties able to make demands before joining the coalition. Dangerous changes to Britain's constitution and parliamentary election rules, now being encouraged by some, are the result of Britain's third party, the Liberal Democrats, being essential to the Conservative party's forming of a ruling coalition (and that, in turn, is the result of the silly TV debates, which – as in America – rewarded a political twit with the celebrity needed to hype his party's share of the vote). America is fortunate to have a two-party system, which, ideally, would have overlapping wings (a left wing of the Republicans overlapping a right wing of the Democrats, which used to be the case). In the U.S. in recent years, these wings have disappeared and a polarization has resulted so that we swing wildly from right to left in presidential changes of parties.

Hopelessly philanthropic efforts to be "fair" to small parties and minority voting blocks, such as "cumulative" voting and other schemes in which third, fourth, fifth or sixth place choices are shuttled around to accommodate minor groups, will undermine democracy and make parliamentary and other governments unstable and gridlocked. First past the post, or majority rule, as we enjoy here, may be heavy-handed, but it works. Early voting is also a mistake – an election should be a snapshot of public opinion at that moment. Having people voting early, months early, is a sham. Only the truly handicapped should vote early or by mail. Moving major elections to a two-day weekend, say the third weekend in October (to avoid bad November weather), would be a help. Voting over a two-day weekend would make it possible for most to get to the polls.

The vision of a Prime Minister Obama having a free hand with all his radical initiatives, is nightmarish. For once, the Senate filibuster, public opinion, Talk Radio, and other curbs on the power of the presidency, seem desperately needed. Consequently, the Madison model is likely to endure far into the future, with its separation of president from the national legislature. But adding the equivalent of a Prime Minister would not be a bad idea.

One way to have a kind of prime minister would be to have the parties choose leaders after each Congressional election. The party leader would have to be a member of the new Congress and would serve two years. The parties would have to choose between candidates from Senate and House and there would have to be some mechanism to allow the leader to assert authority over his rival or rivals in the other house of Congress. During presidential election years the party leader would likely be a candidate for president, though not necessarily carrying any advantage over other members of Congress, business leaders or governors who may also choose to run. The advantage of such a custom would be to endow one person in each party with something like the mantle of a prime minister. It would also put a face on party leadership, in contrast to the leaderless parties of today and it would provide a personal voice for the party. The party would have a leader and that leader would usually be a candidate for president. Another move that would provide a peer-reviewed candidate would be to have Democratic and Republican governors choose one candidate each, from their ranks, as a presidential candidate every four years. Such peer-nominated candidates would be a welcome relief from the gaggle of self-nominated candidates that come out of the woodwork every election cycle. The inescapable lesson is that the party should have a leader and the leader should run for president. He or she may lose to someone else, but should run, anyway. Nearly every major candidate for president since Harry Truman has not been, by any stretch of the imagination, the leader of his or her party.

Some way of firing incompetent presidents, such as through a national referendum, might be considered – given the awful leadership we have been dealt by Carter, Clinton, Bush II, Obama and others. Would a national referendum on the ballot after the first two years (and only then) make sense? It would have rid us of Carter, and possibly of Clinton, but also of Harry Truman, and it would not have created an early retirement for George W. Bush.

What is evident is that the 22nd Amendment was a good idea. It saved us from a possible four terms of Bill Clinton, among other things. Term limits and age limits for members of Congress might help. A sensible retirement limit could be age 75 (putting an end to the spectacle of Strom Thurmond types, still in the Congress at age 100); and a term limit for service could be 24 years (three Senate terms or 12 House terms or some combination of the two). The term limit on service could be lifted for the tiny number of men and women who serve in leadership positions: Speaker of the House, House majority and minority leaders, Senate majority and minority leaders, and their whips. This is a handful of exceptions in a Congress with 535 members, but it would help prevent a wholesale loss of seasoned leadership while simultaneously preventing excessive seniority for most. In addition to term limits and age limits, members of Congress should not have preferential retirement medical insurance programs; at retirement, they should be on Medicare, like most other Americans.

Perhaps the best idea of all is to get better qualified men or women into the White House and the best way to do that is to restore party discipline, rescue the nominating process from television and the showy and often meaningless primaries and their endless TV debates (the best president is not necessarily the best debater), and restore the conventions as the principal means of nominating presidential candidates by reducing by at least half the number of pledged delegates that can be won in primaries. This will require broader participation in politics by the American people, a good example of which has been the Tea Party movement.

The present system has produced such fakers and frauds, such inexperienced and self-serving leaders, that the nation's safety is in peril – for the simple reason that the president has a role, often decisive, in all issues. The presidency itself, cut loose from Congress by the Constitution, has now been cut loose from common purpose and common loyalties. Beginning with Kennedy, it became a glittering bauble, a personal prize, a self-aggrandizing role to play.

The 2011 Republican candidate debates fell into the usual pattern of TV talent show, painfully drawn out by a mad proliferation of the debates, which began in May, 2011, and had reached 16 or so by December, nearly a year ahead of the election. Most of the self-nominated candidates either lacked experience (Herman Cain, Donald Trump, Michele Bachmann), were too far to the right to win a general election (Cain and Bachmann again, plus former U.S. Senator Rick Santorum) were too old (Gingrich, Ron Paul) or were off the charts eccentric (Ron Paul again). Only one popular candidate, Mitt Romney, had any appeal to the independent bloc of voters who now outnumber Democrats and Republicans. In 2011 conservatives in the Republican Party chased after one candidate after another in order to avoid backing Romney. Trump, Bachmann, Governor Rick Perry of Texas, Cain, and finally Newt Gingrich, became the alternatives, each rising and then falling in the polls. Cain, who had no experience in Washington (like Jimmy Carter, his fellow Georgian), saw his campaign unravel as various women came forward with allegations of impropriety on his part. This never hurt Bill Clinton, who simply denied everything as he made his bid for the presidency in 1991-92. The real problem with Cain, though, was a total lack of experience in government – shouldn't Republicans have been thinking about that? Gingrich, if elected, would turn 70 during his first year in office. Like Republican septuagenarians Bob Dole and John McCain, his age would likely cost him the election – the contrast between a dynamic fifty-year-old who looks ten years younger and the portly, aging Gingrich would eclipse all of the latter's debating skills and store of knowledge. Various skeletons in Gingrich's closet would emerge, too, during a presidential campaign – and they did in the primaries.

As in 2008, the independents would be crucial in 2012, a lesson lost on most Republican candidates as they vied with one another for the most strident right wing credentials (end Medicare, slash government indiscriminately, attack collective bargaining, end Social Security as we have known it, push a regressive flat tax that would outrage most voters and, unanimously in a TV debate, reject a hypothetical budget arrangement in which spending cuts outnumbered tax hikes by 10-1). All this nonsense shored up Obama, who went full time into a replay of Harry Truman's 1948 upset victory propaganda line against a "do-nothing Congress," hoping for a similar result in 2012. Several popular and possible Republican candidates wisely stepped aside because of lack of experience (Governor Bob McDonnell of Virginia, Governor Chris Christie of New Jersey and Marco Rubio, recently elected to the U.S. Senate from Florida). This was refreshing but left the field weak. A Zogby poll in late 2011 showed that a near majority of Republicans, independents, and voters at large regarded the Republican field as a poor one. Of the "candidates," only Romney, Gingrich, former Utah governor Jon Huntsman and Perry had anything like the experience a presidential candidate should logically have – and Perry may have made the best observation of all when he pointed out that debating should perhaps not be the primary skill of a president. Harry Truman and Dwight Eisenhower, both top ten presidents in historians' polls, would have been at a significant disadvantage in today's TV debate formats.

The Democrats couldn't put up a single serious candidate

to challenge Barack Obama, one of the weakest and most ineffectual presidents in history, while the Republicans shot up their own tent, as one wag put it, with an ever-proliferating number of shallow TV show debates. The media made the usual circus out of ever-changing polls – the poll changes breathlessly reported by cable and other news channels. Worst of all, the primaries and caucuses were pushed up ever closer to January 1 (the New Hampshire primary, first in the nation, used to be in March).

The Republican debates began almost two years before the election and degenerated into demogagic pitches to the live audiences at the debates, the candidates destroying one another while President Obama looked on approvingly as he built his war chest.

Obviously, this is a dreadful way to select a presidential nominee. Campaigning, debates and primaries should be confined to the election year. Candidates should be nominated by peers or representative party organizations. There should be some connection to party leadership and nominees should have appropriate experience for the job they seek, rather than being motivated entirely by personal ambition or ideological loyalties.

Such a destructive mess was the Republican campaign – and so long was it – that the party probably alienated more voters than it attracted. The British have a three or four week campaign – ours are now being absurdly stretched to two years – and this is because our parties have no leaders to begin with and the conventions are nothing but an afterthought. The ultimate candidate is more often than not a figure of reality television, a celebrity of the moment.

TV news media tend to exaggerate the story of the moment, the sensation of the day. The past is quickly forgotten and the future unanticipated. The moment is everything and the dominant political personality of the moment is Barack Obama, the perpetual campaigner who does little else – which is why he may well defeat any Republican candidate in 2012. A creature of the media, he is little more than media – all image, no substance. He will act his role to the hilt, wrapped as he now is with the presidential mantle – and to the tune of perhaps a billion dollars of TV advertising. The decision to move the Democrat convention in Charlotte from a hall to a stadium for its last day will replicate the messiah-like outdoor extravaganzas that Obama staged in Berlin, Denver, and Chicago in 2008. Politics will remain entertainment – to the detriment of the nation.

THE SECOND CHALLENGE:
OUT OF CONTROL IMMIGRATION

The U.S. immigration crisis has been building for 30 years, yet the three weak presidents, and every Congress serving with them, have avoided dealing with it. The crisis is now so serious that it threatens to fundamentally change America – in negative directions. The population is exploding – from 300 million to 400 million in a few decades, then a rapid rise to half a billion. Almost all the newcomers are non-European, which means the American majority, as in California, will become a minority – quite possibly in only 20 or 30 years. The largest growing segment of the new population is Hispanic (almost entirely from Mexico and Central America) and these immigrants, many of them illegal, are among the poorest, the least skilled and the least educated in American immigration history. Such unskilled labor made sense in the 19th century, when America had plenty of farmland for homesteaders and many factories for employment of the unskilled, but it makes no sense in the technocratic 21st century.

The worst aspect of this rapid Hispanic growth is that the illegitimacy rate in the Hispanic community is skyrocketing – now at about 53% and rising, according to the Pew Hispanic Research Center. Just a decade or two ago, it was in the thirties. This means that the African-American welfare disaster, source of so much poverty, gang activity, crime and drug use, and the chief reason the black American family has collapsed, is now happening over again, but in the much larger and ever-expanding Hispanic community.

How did immigration become such a problem? It is not due to any conspiracy. The problem developed more or less accidentally, and few in either government or the media seem to know how it happened or why.

As most Americans know, a huge wave of immigration swept into America in the late 19th and early 20th centuries. The new immigrants were not primarily from the British Isles or Northwestern Europe, source of most immigrants from 1607 to the 1880s. The new immigrants were from Southern and Eastern Europe and were relatively poor compared to earlier immigrants. They came in such huge numbers that many Americans were alarmed. These were the "huddled masses" of the Ellis Island/Statue of Liberty era and they set an all-time record for a single decade when about nine million showed up 1901-1910. World War I slowed the new immigration and Congress wisely decided to end mass immigration in the early 1920s and to give the nation an immigration breathing spell, a long period in which to assimilate the newcomers. Despite many dire warnings that the newcomers would never be assimilated, over the next half century or so they were. Despite low social standing, poverty and ethnic and sometimes religious differences, the newcomers were largely assimilated into the English-speaking American way of life – and this happened because of *intermarriage*. The new Italian-Jewish-Greek-Slavic immigrants intermarried with the Irish,

German, English, Scotch, Scandinavian Americans already here. The melting pot worked. It was an old joke that Serbs and Croats killed one another in Yugoslavia but married one another in Chicago. The American melting pot overcame ethnic differences. Even Jews, with a differing religion, eventually saw half their marriages cross ethnic lines. But it took a half century breathing spell, roughly from the 1920s to the 1970s, to effect this assimilation. By coincidence, the Great Depression and the Second World War would have reduced immigration anyway – but Congress did the right thing in the 1920s.

Unfortunately, from the point of view of many, Congress, in the 1920s, also set ethnic quotas for new immigrants. Desiring to keep America an Anglo-European country they set "national origins" quotas based on the 1890 census (which obviously favored Germany, Northwestern Europe and the British Isles – old stock Americans). The acts specifically forbade immigration from Asia and drastically reduced immigration from Eastern Europe (which would have fateful consequences much later). Interestingly, the restrictive immigration laws did not apply to Mexico or Latin America, in part because Mexicans came and went as labor needs demanded or internal Mexican politics or pressures dictated. The new laws also drastically reduced overall immigrant numbers – to under 200,000 per year (the historic average has been, until recently, about 250,000 annually). This contrasted with the amazing figure of 1.3 million immigrants in a single year – 1907.

The rescinding of these "national origins" rules was inevitable and became a crusade in the 1960s for the Kennedy brothers – John, Robert and Ted, themselves great-grandchildren of Irish immigrants. An important point to note is that quotas and restrictions are inevitable as there are millions of people around the world who have legally applied to immigrate to the United States. If the U.S. had no restrictions many times that number would flood in. A recent poll in Mexico showed that about half the population of 120 million would prefer to live in the U.S. and a third of them would come illegally if they could. Legal immigration to the U.S. today is running at or somewhat over one million a year – an all-time high.

John F. Kennedy did not live to see an end to national origins restrictions but his brothers, both U.S. Senators at the time, managed to get an immigration reform bill passed in 1965 that effectively ended the national origins quotas and, inadvertently, created the issues for today's immigration debate.

Sen. Ted Kennedy (Massachusetts) claimed that the changes to the 1920s statutes would not bring in a million immigrants annually, nor would they substantially change the overall ethnic mix of immigrants. The idea was to re-open the door to Eastern Europeans, to open the door to Asians, and to allow more legal immigrants from the Western Hemisphere. Nevertheless, overall numbers were kept at a modest 300,000 a year, not counting sponsorship of blood relatives under a "family reunification" provision. Kennedy was spectacularly wrong, of course, and the unintended consequences of his bill have helped create today's crisis.

Two important consequences were not foreseen: first, that Eastern Europeans would not be able to take advantage of the new friendliness of our immigration laws for the very obvious reason that, in the 1960s (and really until about 1990), they were trapped in Communist countries and couldn't get out; second, that the family reunification would create huge "family chains" for those first through the door in 1965 and after – which proved especially true of Mexicans and Filipinos. The new law let in, as sponsored immigrants, parents, brothers and sisters, married children, plus other relatives. Almost immediately, yearly totals began to soar, eventually tripling the overall numbers of 1965. The law was creating a tidal wave of relatives of relatives of relatives, an outcome not foreseen by Kennedy or others in Congress who voted for it.

Overall legal immigration in the decade of the 1960s was 3.3 million; in the 1970s, 4.5 million; in the 1980s, 7.3 million; in the 1990s, an all-time record 9 million, with 1.8 million in the single year, 1991. The decade 2001-2010 has topped the 1990s record. More importantly, these figures *have been matched or exceeded* by illegal immigration from Mexico and Central America, which has been running at a half million to a million or more each year for decades. *Time* magazine estimated that in a single year over 4 million Hispanics crossed our borders – although many, no doubt, were counted going both ways. At present over 10% of all Mexicans born in Mexico live legally or illegally in the U.S. Tens of billions of dollars of income (that Americans would spend here) are being sent back to Mexico each year. Legal and illegal immigration has become an important part of the Mexican economy. Recently, the sheriff of Pinal County on the Arizona/Mexican border, revealed that 90,000 illegals per month enter Arizona in his county alone – over a million a year. By contrast, the entire legal immigration numbers from all of Europe run to a meager 160,000 per year – though millions would come if they had but to walk across an undefended border. In addition to these legal and illegal immigrants from Mexico and Central America, some 200,000 or more "anchor babies" are born in the U.S. each year (65,000 in Texas alone) – these are children of illegal aliens who are automatically granted U.S. citizenship via a philanthropic reading of the Fourteenth Amendment – which was intended to insure that African-American slaves were counted as citizens because they were born on U.S. soil. To give some idea of what an unprecedented tidal wave of Hispanics we have had in recent decades, the number of anchor babies alone nearly matches the average yearly total for *all* immigrants admitted yearly throughout our history.

The result of these developments is that immigration to the U.S. is not at the 300,000 annual mark set in 1965, but – legal and illegal - is running at five or six times that number. Half of all legal immigration comes from south of the border, including the Caribbean, and almost all illegal immigration is from the same areas. Because of the family chains, Latino and East Asian immigrants dominate legal immigration, with Latinos far in the lead. In an average year, more Mexicans become U.S. citizens than do immigrants from all 40 European countries combined. Democrats and country club Republicans have been pushing for a second amnesty for illegal aliens (the first was in 1986). The number of such illegals has been estimated by some sources at 12 million, but it could easily be as high as 20 million. If it is 12 million, it would take 75 years, at the rate Europeans are coming in legally now, to equal an amnesty of 12 million Hispanics. Various think tanks, including the Heritage Foundation, estimate that an amnesty for 12 million Hispanics would actually increase the American Hispanic population by 30 to 60 million within a generation or two, due to high birth rates and family chain consequences.

The 1986 amnesty for about 3 million Hispanic illegals had the unintended effect of delivering California to the Democratic Party more or less in perpetuity. California used to be in play, politically, for Republicans, who regularly had governors and U.S. Senators elected there and who had two California Republicans, Richard Nixon and Ronald Reagan, make it to the White House. Today, the state legislature, the state's House Congressional delegation and both U.S. Senators are Democrat-dominated, with all that means in terms of the state's record number of presidential electoral votes.

An amnesty of 12 to 20 million would set the Democrats up for domination of every major American super state – Florida, New York, Texas and California – and keep their party in power indefinitely. For all practical purposes, the two-party system in the United States would be dead.

Because of the family chain, the Philippines, Mexico and China have a big advantage in numbers and East Asians, overall, a big advantage over West Asians (people from India, Pakistan, Bangladesh, etc.). The new immigration is not "global," as many politicians insist – it all but ignores large areas of the world: Europe, South America, Africa. It would be interesting and even beneficial if a fifth or so of our legal immigrants were really global – taking in the best and brightest from everywhere, regardless of race or religion, and adding a global fringe to the national garment. But that is not what is happening. In essence, we have been experiencing an enormous wave of nearby Hispanics and a smaller wave of East Asians, with no regard for the consequences – cultural, social or political.

It should be noted that Asian immigrants have done exceedingly well in the United States, as their numbers have risen since the 1970s. They have the lowest crime and divorce rates, and the highest educational and income levels of all groups in the U.S. Like the Jewish immigrants from Eastern Europe in the great 19th century wave, they are enriching and improving their new country. It would make perfect sense to keep Asian immigration figures about where they are now – with, perhaps, some adjustments in fairness to those who have been nudged out (Indonesians, Burmese, Thai) and to balance East and West Asians by letting in a larger percentage of the whole from West Asia (India and its neighbors). It is true that some Asian groups (Cambodians, Laotians) have not done as well as others (Chinese, Japanese), but overall Asians have done very well here.

Asian intermarriage rates (by the third generation) were once encouraging, with Asian marriage rates with non-Asians at around 40%, by the third generation – higher for Filipinos. But recent studies show a sharp drop in intermarriage, a disturbing trend. Helpful to Asian cultural assimilation is the multiplicity of languages among these immigrants. Unlike Hispanics they speak many languages, and that creates a strong incentive to learn English as a common language. Nevertheless, Asians do stand apart somewhat and are almost invisible in popular culture – movies, TV shows, advertising.

There may be increasing demands from them for change in these areas.

Illegal immigration also derives from overstayed visas, now estimated at 300,000 a year. Most of these are also Hispanics, according to various studies. Overstaying visas is an international problem – even Japan has some 100,000 people a year overstaying visas. The U.S. government is woefully undermanned when it comes to supervising visas and apprehending those who have overstayed. Similarly, the U.S. does not have anything like the number of detention centers, judges and lawyers, agents and others who are involved in apprehending those who have crossed our borders illegally. In general, the U.S. attitude toward the phenomenon has been passive and ineffective, whether the illegals crossed the border or simply overstayed visas. Newspaper and media stories on the issue, even in conservative states, are invariably written from the philanthropic point of view, concentrating on a single family or a distressed individual. The larger picture always seems to escape the reporters who write them – and the editors who order the stories.

One of the fascinating aspects of this entire situation is how the media reports it as a *fait accompli*. It has to happen. The press regularly reports that the U.S. population will escalate to 400 million by 2050 (or even 2040) as if it were an incontrovertible fact. Similarly, the press announces that Anglo-Americans will be a minority by such and such a date. That's it – nothing can be done. Never is there any mention of the fact that these things are happening because of Congressional action (or inaction) and that the results can be changed if Congress has the will to effect the change.

First, there is no sensible reason why the American majority should become a minority. No one has asked Anglo-Americans if they want to be a minority in a few decades. There has been no public debate on the issue – and there obviously should be. Nor has there been any debate on overpopulation. We are headed for 400 million, then 500 million, then 600 million – and not a peep from the hypocrites in the environmental movement, notably the Sierra Club in California, which is at ground zero of uncontrolled population growth due to the Latino invasion. The Sierra Club executive board, in a majority, is paralyzed by political correctness on this issue. California, with an estimated three million illegal aliens – most of them Mexican – is staggering under a load of debt that threatens state bankruptcy. But not a word from responsible parties – and the Roman Catholic Church there staunchly favors the illegals, seemingly accepting a never-ending invasion as virtue while exhibiting no insight into the harm being done to California, its environment, and its citizens. The greatest movement of people *out of* an American state occurred in California in the 1990s when millions of white and black Americans left the state, while millions of legal and illegal Hispanics and Asians moved in. That record withdrawal was topped in the next decade. Nevertheless, despite the exodus, there is a very real possibility that if nothing is done to stop it, California's population could double to 70 million in just a few decades – yet environmental groups there are silent.

Historically, America has been an Anglo-European country with a sizable African-American minority that ranged, over the centuries, from 12 to 20 per cent. The enormous, unprecedented increase in non-European immigration, legal and illegal, from the 1970s to today – while Europeans were more or less kept out – dramatically reduced the Anglo-European portion of the population. If nothing is done, the Anglo-European population will drop below 50% by 2040 or so, as it already has in California. Culturally, the splitting of America into huge ethnic/racial blocks may affect films, TV programming, literature, plays, music and the like. It is less likely that the nation will experience a shared popular culture, as in the past. Niche TV viewing is likely. Hispanics watching their cable channels in Spanish, others theirs. This splintering of the population will also lead, inevitably, to demands for quotas – so many Hispanics on the Supreme Court, so many Asians in TV ads, so many blacks on city councils or corporate boards. Each group will feel left out and a sense of America as a genuine historic community with a common culture and language may be lost. What, for example, will all the movies, plays and novels of the past – dominated by white people – mean to the non-whites who dominate America numerically in the future? The cries for "multiculturalism," already a problem, will increase, along with strident claims for proper representation in almost everything imaginable. But remember, the growth in minorities is not "global" or balanced in any way. It is overwhelmingly dominated by Spanish-speaking Hispanics from Mexico and Central America and to a lesser degree by East Asians. Almost no immigrants are coming from the more European nations of South America: Argentina, Uruguay, Chile – nor from Portuguese-speaking Brazil. Very few Eastern Europeans are being allowed in, though millions would come if allowed. Midwestern states, many losing population or standing still, would welcome

Eastern European immigrants, whose children born here would be indistinguishable from most Midwestern children. If Midwestern governors had any sense, they would long ago have agitated for more European immigrants – but that would be a gross violation of political correctness and the cowardice it engenders. Because of the lopsided nature of legal and illegal immigration, the American future, if nothing is done, is not so much "multicultural" or "global," as it is Hispanic and Mexican.

Another irrationality favoring Mexican growth in the U.S. is birthright citizenship ("anchor babies"), as noted. The Fourteenth Amendment to the U.S. Constitution states that "All persons born or naturalized in the U.S. ... are Citizens of the U.S. and of the state wherein they reside." This was passed after the conclusion of the American Civil War to insure that black slaves, now freed, would be granted full citizenship. What no one at the time anticipated was the possibility that hundreds of thousands of Mexicans would cross the border to deliver their babies on U.S. soil, thus earning American citizenship for them. This is now happening and the three weak presidents and their attendant Congresses have – as with so many problems, issues and crises – done nothing to repair the situation. A baby citizen, if the family has an immigration lawyer, can, over time, be used to sponsor or bring in the parents and other relatives. Given the wording of the Fourteenth Amendment, it may be necessary to pass a constitutional amendment to change the situation, though Congress could pass a law as a court test first. The usual human rights organizations and Mexican advocacy groups will cry foul, but it is obviously something that should have been addressed long ago.

So far, immigrants from Mexico and Central America have been learning English by the third generation, repeating the historic experience of other immigrant groups, but that was with the smaller numbers of yesteryear. The avalanche of illegal aliens just in the past few decades, with tens of millions arriving – many through the empty spaces of Arizona – may alter that pattern. As historian Samuel Huntington pointed out in *Who Are We?*, the more Hispanics converge in areas already saturated by Hispanic migration, the more likely they are to marry each other – and, perhaps, the more likely they are to continue speaking Spanish and not only in the home. The demand to make Spanish a co-official language of the U.S. is inevitable if the tidal wave is not stopped. We would become as bedeviled as Canada and Belgium, both of which are officially two-language nations and both of which have almost split apart as a result. If Congress doesn't vote Spanish as a co-equal language the courts will, given the activism that will result from Hispanic political pressures and Democrat domination of court appointments.

In his book, *The Democratic Experience* (with Paul Sigmund, 1969), the famous American theologian, Reinhold Niebuhr, pointed out the dangers that diversity in race and language pose to stable democracy and a strong sense of community. A common ethnicity and a common language, in his view, were prerequisites for the rise of democracy in European states and preceded political democracy by centuries. The unraveling of commonality will fracture our sense of togetherness and of community.

The last point touches on the most profound change of all: politics. Hispanics, like blacks, tend to vote Democrat.

American blacks began voting majority Democrat during the 1960s, following passage of the landmark civil rights bills (despite that Republicans had supported the bills and most opposition had come from Southern Democrats). Gradually, decade to decade for blacks, the percentage of the Democrat vote has increased as welfare dependency has increased. Welfare mothers vote overwhelmingly Democrat and many black children are on welfare. This has brought the Democrat share of the black vote to about 90% (95% for Barack Obama). Hispanics have been voting, on average, about 2-1 Democrat, though the numbers have ranged from 58% to 75% in major elections. In no recent presidential election has the Republican candidate done much better than 43% of the Hispanic vote – and that is a landslide loss. George W. Bush, an assiduous pursuer of the Hispanic vote throughout his political career, lost the Hispanic vote in California 3-1 in his 2000 presidential race. He "won" the rest of the country by more than half a million votes, but lost California by over a million, thus creating the myth that Al Gore "won" the presidency by more than half a million votes nationally. In 2008 the Hispanic vote had an even more dramatic impact in California: Barack Obama won the state by over three million votes, fully a third of his national plurality. Politically, California is leaving the United States. Like Scotland in Great Britain and Quebec in Canada, California votes so lopsidedly against one of the major two parties as to skew national results and all but remove itself from the two-party system.

For all practical purposes, American blacks do not participate in a two-party system or in a real democracy. They come forward and vote plebiscite fashion, as do voters in Cuba and Venezuela, or, historically, in Mussolini's Italy. Hispanics bid to follow their example. As illegitimacy and welfare rates go up, so does the Democrat share of the vote.

As mentioned, George W. Bush emulated his father (George H.W. Bush) and brother (Jeb Bush, governor of Florida) in seeking Hispanic support. But in two Texas gubernatorial runs and two presidential runs, he lost the Hispanic vote in all four races at landslide levels. The younger Bush seemed almost obsessed with pleasing Mexican public opinion, Mexican presidents, and Mexican-American voters. He did absolutely nothing effective about the border crisis for eight years, vastly increasing the illegal population in the U.S., and his first state guest at the White House was not Tony Blair, Prime Minister of Britain and our staunchest ally, but Vicente Fox, the president of Mexico, who wouldn't even support us in UN voting on Iraq and other issues. At the time, Bush said that no country was more important to the U.S. than Mexico, sidestepping the obvious fact that no country is more of a problem than Mexico and no country is more important to us than Britain.

Members of Bush's inner circle have always pumped up the Hispanic voting figures for Bush. In his second gubernatorial run, they claimed Bush won 44% of the Hispanic vote. A careful check in Spanish-speaking precincts showed it was more like 41%. He did get 43% of the Hispanic vote in his second presidential run after showing how weak he was on border security and immigration reform. These better showings were still landslide losses – and it doesn't take a PhD to see that the larger the number of Hispanic voters the bigger that slice at 60-40 is for the Democrats. Even a 52-48 split –

four points – would be telling if the Hispanic voting pie grows ever larger. Fifteen or sixteen per cent of an ever larger voting pool is a killer for Republicans, yet "winning the Hispanic vote" has been the folly behind country club Republican refusal to do anything meaningful about immigration reform. If only we let in enough of them and are weak enough on the issue, the reasoning is, they will see the light and vote for us. Instead, Hispanics tend to vote as a bloc, and for government subsidies, and will no doubt continue to do so.

To put it bluntly, an ever-growing Hispanic population means the end of the two-party system and the elevation of Democrats to majority status far longer than the Great Depression-influenced period of 1930-94 – and it will be more complete, as it will undoubtedly mean governorships and legislatures in all the larger states, both houses of Congress and nearly every president. California, Arizona, Texas, Florida, Illinois, Michigan and New York could be dominated by new minority majorities – a fact well understood by Barack Obama, who is doing all he can to bring it about. One can't help but wonder what the response of Obama and his political allies would be to a recommendation to offset the 12 million poor they wish to amnesty (mostly potential Democrat voters) with 12 million affluent people from around the world, who might be expected to vote 2-1 Republican after taking up residence here. Obama has even spoken in his inner circle about the outrageous possibility of providing amnesty for millions of illegals via a presidential pardon or parole. He refuses to do anything about Arizona's desperate situation unless Republicans agree to a citizenship amnesty so he can revolutionize American politics and keep his party in power indefinitely. Worse, he has set his Justice Department against Arizona, Alabama and Georgia, to kill immigration reform measures passed by their legislatures, measures that often echo federal ones that Obama refuses to enforce (thus violating his oath of office).

In addition to these negative results, overwhelming Hispanic migration is also too regional. Unlike the Anglo-European immigration patterns of previous centuries, which fanned out across the entire country from Maine to California, Hispanic migration is largely concentrated in states close to Mexico, especially Texas and California. Much of the nation doesn't understand what the fuss is about because the crisis isn't happening in Wisconsin, New Hampshire, Pennsylvania, Minnesota, Montana, Oregon or Wyoming to anything like the degree it is in California, Arizona, Texas and Florida.

Because of the very obvious exception for Hispanics – that their mother country is on our border (and 2,000 miles of it) –there is much concern over whether they will intermarry with other Americans as Italian, German, Scandinavian, Irish and other immigrants did in the past. Earlier arrivals, including recent Asian immigrants, had to cross oceans to get here. The mother countries were not a day's drive away – complete with electronic magnification of a readily accessible Spanish language culture via radio and television. Studies show, as Huntington pointed out, that Hispanic intermarriage rates are low – and lower by the fourth generation. Though controversial, some studies suggest intermarriage rates no higher than 30% by the third generation and as low as 15% in some surveys. As a result, instead of Hispanics blending into the U.S. melting pot, we have something like Mexico extending itself into the United States. The distinguished historian, Victor Davis Hanson, a lifelong resident of California's Central Valley agricultural region, has written of entire counties that have now sunk into Third World levels of maintenance, where the populations are 95% Mexican, with high levels of poverty and illiteracy.

Crime is yet another problem with open borders. It is estimated that 90% of the heroin, cocaine and methamphetamine coming into the U.S. crosses the open Mexican border. Vicious criminal gangs from Central America and Mexico have set up shop in the U.S. A few years ago, the *Los Angeles Times* ran a major investigating piece on criminal gangs in Los Angeles. They estimated the number of gang members at over 70,000 (the police force was about 13,000 then), with Hispanics the largest group, then blacks, then Asians. At that time the city population of about three million was half non-Hispanic white. The number of white gang members was estimated at 400. Half the city was providing 400 gang members, while the minority half was providing 70,000! Even if the figures were off by a wide margin, the contrast is stark.

Mexico itself is enduring a horrific crime wave that has killed over 47,000 people in the past five years (nine times our eight-year war casualties in Iraq). Drug lords are at war with one another and with the federal government. Victims are being tortured, beheaded, slaughtered, all along the U.S. border and the violence is lapping over into American towns and cities. Phoenix now leads the nation in kidnappings and, along with Mexico City, is one of the leading kidnapping locations in the world. The legal and illegal immigrants are bringing some of that crime into the U.S. Worse, the Border Patrol has captured many illegal immigrants from Middle Eastern countries who have entered the U.S. via the Mexican border. It is a certainty that terrorists have made it safely into the U.S. in this fashion.

Those who favor open borders and an endless Hispanic invasion – even the merging of Central America and Mexico with the U.S. (*The Wall Street Journal*, almost every Hispanic advocacy group, the Democratic Party, etc.) – argue that we are, after all, "a nation of immigrants." As Huntington points out, that is not true. Most Americans, over the centuries, have been born here – they are the children, grandchildren or great-grandchildren of immigrants – or are even further removed from the initial immigrant wave. In general there have been four great waves of immigrants: the original Anglo-Irish founding wave in the 17th and 18th centuries; an Irish-German wave in the mid-19th century; an enormous Eastern European wave a decade or two either way of 1900; and the Latino/Asian wave from the 1970s to the present. So huge is the present wave that we have probably exceeded the all-time record level of foreign born, which was about 15% in 1910. Even then, obviously, 85% of Americans had been born in the United States. The vast majority of Americans, now and in the past, have not been immigrants: they have been citizens born and raised in an English-speaking, predominantly European culture. Almost no one seems to know it now, but when the U.S. helped found NATO in 1949 and drew up its protocols, one of them was a call of loyalty to "European culture," which America was understood to share. Imagine the horror that would be expressed by the busy multiculturalists and "diversity" zealots if such a treaty were signed today.

Another argument is that only heavy immigration will provide enough workers to pay for future Social Security and Medicare costs. The problem is that the number to achieve that would be so huge we would have to go over the billion mark in population to keep up; obviously, other remedies will have to be found. The truth is rather the reverse: Medicaid and Medicare costs will go up because of the general poverty and lack of education and job skills that characterizes the Hispanic immigrant community. The U.S. Federal government and nearly all the states (especially those impacted by immigration) are struggling desperately to meet the burden of present Medicaid costs (yet President Obama and the Democrat party, on a strict party-line vote, have passed Obamacare, which will enormously increase these same costs).

But even if it were true that immigration would help meet these costs, why would all or most of the population growth have to be Hispanic? This last is the same answer to the notion that we need Hispanics to do the work Americans won't do. This has always been a false argument for it is not the jobs that Americans won't do, it's the low wages they won't accept. Contrary to the myth that Hispanics are mostly working in agricultural or food processing work, one of their largest areas of employment is construction, where Hispanics work at two thirds or less of the wage scale of Americans. In food processing plants in Kansas, Nebraska and Iowa, they are working for wages, adjusted for inflation, that are *lower* than those of Americans in similar plants 30 years ago.

Unskilled immigrants make for cheap labor, which is why their importation has been so popular with various business groups, the U.S. Chamber of Commerce, and cheap labor Republicans like former Nebraska Senator Chuck Hagel and South Carolina Senator Lindsey Graham. As some have wisely put it, the Latino invasion is all about cheap votes for Democrats and cheap labor for Republicans. But even if it were true that Hispanics will do jobs Americans won't, every one of those jobs could go to a non-Hispanic immigrant. Mexico's per capita income, though only one seventh that of the U.S., is two or three times that of Ukraine. There are plenty of Ukrainians, Poles, Serbs, Croats, Bosnians and Russians who do the same lowly jobs in their countries that many Hispanics do here – and they would jump at the chance to immigrate to the U.S. for those same jobs. The same could be said for Pakistanis and Indians, who would drop everything to come here for such employment.

The notion that Anglo-Americans should roll over and accept minority status in a new "multicultural" America is as foolish as the notion that the Irish, four million strong, would accept the suggestion that they should become a minority in their own country. It takes a long time for a national togetherness, a national culture, to form, but when it does you have something like modern France or modern Japan. Centuries ago, Japan was riven by divisions and France was a jumble of peoples speaking various dialects. But today they are recognizably homogenous nations and neither the French nor the Japanese (or the Irish) would welcome minority status within their own countries. Imagine telling the Irish they had to import five million Arabs so that there would be a new ethnic majority and a new majority religion. This would be an insane suggestion rejected by nearly everyone in Ireland except the small number of deathwishers they undoubtedly harbor somewhere (probably in academia).

Another argument in favor of the Hispanic invasion is the hoary one that we need more diversity. Never mind that America is already one of the most diverse nations in the world, but consider what diversity did for Yugoslavia. The former Communist country, held together by an authoritarian government after World War II, has celebrated its diversity by splitting into seven regions, during which breakup over 100,000 people were killed in ethnic and religious conflict. Seven ethnic groups, three religions, and two alphabets split the country asunder. Yugoslavia is not alone – ethnic and linguistic minorities are tearing apart countries in every part of the world, including civilized Belgium. There is a great deal to be said for homogeneity – but it is not politically correct to do so.

Philanthropy and permissiveness, the hallmarks of the upper class, make a perfect fit with the do-nothing, open borders situation we've had for decades. The attitude of the elites is always one of sympathy and compassion (which neatly covers their political and economic self interests). Press and media echo those attitudes, only rarely pointing out the problems, costs, and difficulties posed by runaway legal and illegal immigration. The elites wish to be open-minded about mass immigration, legal and illegal. But as has often been said, while it is good to be open-minded, it is not good to be so open-minded that your brains fall out.

The mass of Mexican-Americans cheering for a Mexican

soccer team playing in Los Angeles while booing the American team, made a deep impression on many. Vast crowds of Mexicans and Hispanics demonstrating in our streets waving Mexican flags gives us pause. The hysterical reaction among American Hispanics to the mild, certainly ineffective Arizona law that police, if they pick someone up for cause, should also check their immigration status, is another indication that tribal loyalties based on language, race and ethnicity may be stronger than the bonds Hispanics have to the country that so generously let them in and allows them to stay. The Obama administration's response to the rather tepid Arizona law with a lawsuit challenging its "constitutionality" is a clear indication of how radical this administration is (the Arizona law is weaker than a similar federal law that Obama's government is supposed to be enforcing).

Another fraud is the H1-B program which has brought in tens of thousands of foreign workers in virtual indentured servitude to take away technical jobs from Americans, but at lower wages. Urged on by high tech business leaders like Bill Gates of Microsoft, Congress authorized non-immigrant visas for foreign workers (lasting three to six years) who are bound by contract to certain employers and certain wage levels. The idea is that America doesn't have enough technical workers (which is not true) and foreign imports are necessary. Like the foolish claim that America was falling far behind Soviet Russia in "engineers and scientists" in the 1950s, the latest claims are false. The entire program is largely an effort to import foreign workers at low wage levels to supplant qualified Americans. U.S. community colleges and universities are pouring out high numbers of computer tech graduates, which gives the lie to Gates' claims. There was a period of several years when it was difficult for qualified Americans to find employment in technical computer-related fields because so many Indians and Pakistanis had come in under the H1-B programs. Beware the calls for huge numbers of immigrants needed for our industries – these calls usually come from elitist billionaires such as Gates and New York mayor Michael Bloomberg.

America has always allowed in the super brightest – the crème de la crème – but run of the mill technicians from India and Pakistan we do not need. Another falsehood is that we need an ongoing Mexican "guestworker" program for seasonal agricultural jobs. We have some 50 million Mexicans and other Hispanics in our country now – and total agricultural worker needs are less than two million. There shouldn't be a problem. Also, Congress, over a period of decades, has passed numerous agricultural worker programs for seasonal and temporary employment. Why haven't they worked?

Much has been made of the "comprehensive" immigration reform favored by the elites – Democrats and country club Republicans. The word "comprehensive" is a red flag that the bill is phony and that it will do little to stop the flow of illegals but will do a lot to provide amnesty for millions of them. There was a typical comprehensive bill in 1986: it amnestied three million illegal aliens (mostly Mexicans) and delivered the state of California to the Democrats, but did nothing effective to stop mass illegal immigration. George W. Bush was always in favor of another comprehensive bill and in 2006 and 2007 a bill co-sponsored by Sen. John McCain of Arizona and Ted Kennedy (probably the worst ever political figure on immigration issues), was pushed hard by the Bush White House. The bill would have provided amnesty, a worker ID card (notoriously easy to fake), and "a path to citizenship" for the estimated 12 million illegals (thus killing the Republican Party, an obvious fact Bush overlooked).

President Obama has now taken up the "comprehensive" banner, while saying that our borders are "too vast" to be effectively policed. This provides a loud clue as to how little he will do for border security after he gets his political amnesty from Congress. The 1986 amnesty was supposed to be part of a "comprehensive" solution, too, but only the amnesty part was implemented.

"Path to citizenship" is one of the agitrop lines used by pro-amnesty supporters, as is "out of the shadows," another agitrop line intended to gain sympathy. Communist parties used to publish these "agitrop" lines as a guide to their knee jerk followers world-wide. The phrase is short for "agitation-propaganda," an open admission that lies were to be accepted as working truths in order to advance party interests. In recent years, the Democratic Party has been given to these agitrop exercises, dubbed "talking points" in the U.S. On Sunday TV political talk shows one can hear a series of Democrats on different programs all echoing the same party line in exactly the same words – making it easy for Rush Limbaugh and other radio talk show hosts to splice together tapes in which the ridiculousness of the habit is pilloried. "Comprehensive immigration reform" is just as dishonest as "a path to citizenship" and "out of the shadows." Beware these phrases, all of which are now being employed by President Obama, who is deliberately holding up any meaningful border security measures until he can force Congress to provide the citizenship amnesty that will help create the huge Democrat voting majority he seeks. Even then, it is doubtful that he or his party would ever really close the border to illegals. He is basically an "open borders" president.

The "comprehensive" bill of 2007 failed in part because angry Americans flooded Congressional phone and fax lines, actually shutting down the Senate phone system. In fact, the bill passed on a 53-47 vote in the Senate, but that vote was not enough to overcome a Republican filibuster (what little has been done to stop immigration madness has been accomplished by Republicans, it should be noted). If passed, the bill – largely a backroom deal brokered by its sponsors with Senate majority leader, Harry Reid – would have provided amnesty and eventual citizenship while doing next to nothing to close the border. It also would have legalized an ongoing "guestworker" program – probably the worst aspect of the bill, for it would have legalized a never-ending cheap labor Latino invasion of the United States at the expense of those worldwide who have legally filed for immigration acceptance and who have patiently waited years or decades to be allowed in. The ongoing guestworker provision, which the Democrats still want today (and some Republicans, too including, unfortunately, Newt Gingrich), contra all common sense – would hasten all the unpleasant aspects and destructive long term results outlined above. Ongoing guestworker programs would depress wages and continue all the problems associated with the invasion.

Obviously, had the comprehensive bill passed, it would have been an enormous incentive to another 12 million to come rushing across the border. The number of border patrol guards in 2007 was only 16,000 and most of the border fencing ordered by a Republican Congress in 2006 (against the wishes of Republican president Bush) had not yet been constructed. The border fencing was for only 600 miles or so of the 2,000 mile border and has still not been completed as a double layer fence – much of it is simply vehicle obstacles or single layer fencing easy to violate (it is the lowest of low priorities for Barack Obama). The "virtual fence" touted by politicians in both parties, has been scrapped after millions were wasted on it. It simply didn't work.

President Bush had a welcome opportunity after 9/11 to close the border for security reasons. Congress would then have very likely funded fencing for much of the border plus a substantive increase in the Border Patrol, but, incredibly, Bush left the border wide open for the next seven years. Even most Mexican-Americans would probably have understood the need to close the border after 9/11. Bush's deliberate failure to push for such a reform was typical of his Mexico-first outlook and his natural tendency toward procrastination. Bush was so irrationally devoted to pleasing Mexico that he had two U.S. border guards charged under the Rico statute after they shot a fleeing Mexican drug runner in the posterior. Bush assigned one of his top prosecutors, Johnny Sutton, to railroad these men (both of them Mexican-Americans, incidentally) into prison, where one of them was kept in solitary confinement (for his own security, but painful, nonetheless), when a lesser penalty should have accrued due to their dereliction in reporting the incident honestly. This cruelty was exercised to placate Mexican public opinion and to send a strong signal to the Mexican government that Bush was on their side. Eventually, during his last days in office and under tremendous pressure from his own party, he commuted the remainder of their sentences, but refused to pardon them. The Mexican government registered its anger at the commutation.

With the dramatic exceptions of his 9/11 response (attacking Afghanistan) and his invasion of Iraq in 2003, Bush was essentially a do-nothing president, timid and out of touch – and extraordinarily poor in communicating with the American people. The sad fact is that Bush's "comprehensive" bill is now Obama's approach – you will hear the same agitrop phrases from him. Sen. McCain, to his credit, finally got the message – close the border first – but he is still talking about an ongoing "guestworker" program, which is sad.

Of the three recent weak presidents, the one who did the most on immigration reform was Bill Clinton – and he deserves credit for that. Clinton approved a very effective fencing measure around San Diego when that area was being overrun, as the Tucson area is now. According to the Border Patrol, the extensive fencing, which extends even into the water, was more than 90% effective in stopping the invasion there. Little remembered today was his surprising decision in 1995 to endorse the immigration proposals that the dynamic black Democrat Congresswoman Barbara Jordan proposed as chair of a Congressional Commission on immigration reform. The Jordan Commission reforms, if carried out, would have reduced the flow of *legal* unskilled Latino labor into the U.S. by over 200,000 a year. It would also have put stiff penalties on employers of illegal aliens and would have established a national identity card. It would also have tightened family reunification and demanded better job skills for legal immigrants. This was before the Democratic Party and its allied labor unions concluded that Hispanic immigration was the only way to grow their voting and membership rolls. In those days, and previously, the Democratic Party had led the fight against cheap immigrant labor in order to protect American jobs and salaries. Despite a front page story in *USA Today* and the support of Clinton, the bill was killed in Congress by politicians like Spencer Abraham, a cheap labor Republican and an Arab-American in favor of *increasing* immigration numbers. Clinton did not stop the overall invasion, but he showed more common sense on the issue than Bush II and Obama, both of whom have been unashamed open borders advocates.

The sorry response to this crisis by Congress and recent presidents stands in stark contrast to the response of President Eisenhower in the 1950s. Alarmed at a big increase in Mexican illegal immigration, Eisenhower mobilized the federal government, in cooperation with state and local police and other agencies, to drive an estimated one million illegals out of the U.S. (most went on their own accord because of the pressures from government). The project was dubbed "Operation Wetback." Imagine the outcry from rights groups and from church groups if anything like that was attempted today! But it worked – and it was legal and correct and in the best interests of the United States.

What can be done today? Obviously, close the border first. Where fencing and walls have been formidable (as near San Diego) they have worked. Essentially, it's an engineering problem and one we are more than up to. Wall up most of the border, with check points at strategic spots, and increase the Border Patrol to 50,000 or so, to enable them to back up the wall. Forget about "virtual fencing," drones and other gimmicks. We need a barrier and we need men behind the barrier.

Forget, also, about "citizenship amnesty" for the 12 to 20 million illegals, but consider some kind of "workplace amnesty." But do this only after closing the border effectively and doing some squeezing via workplace inspections and pressures. Attrition will send some of the 12 million back home. Some illegals, though, have been here a long time and have children born here who are American citizens. Sending them away from their children, breaking up families, would be cruel and unnecessary.

Any attempt to forcibly evict 12 million people would set off riots, street marches, and, in general, the biggest civil rights convulsion in American history. The liberal church groups, including the Roman Catholic Church, would staunchly support the Hispanic "victims" and the effort to evict would fail miserably, and impose huge political costs on the government that attempted it. Besides, the U.S. government doesn't have the manpower or resources to identify and evict 12 million people.

Having a few million foreign "guestworkers" would be, proportionately, a fairly normal thing for an advanced country – almost every European country, including highly civilized Switzerland, has foreign guestworkers. This *does not mean an ongoing guestworker program*. It means a one-time-only acceptance of employed guestworkers already here – and this cannot be done until step one, the closing of the border, has been certified as successful, and step two, workplace enforcement pressures, have been stepped up via E-Verify or other means. Even then, not every illegal would qualify as a guestworker. Job skills, full time employment, parenting of children born here, length of stay, would all have to be considered. Continued use – in fact, expanded use – of the E-Verify program would be necessary because so many illegals have stolen the Social Security numbers of American citizens.

There would be no citizenship amnesty and no path to voting – for all the reasons cited above. However, anyone can go back to their country of origin and apply to immigrate to the U.S. If they do so, they will have to go to the end of the line (behind the millions already registered globally) and wait – and wait. Many of them would never make it, but some would. That is only fair to those in other parts of the world who have legally registered to emigrate. The foreign guestworkers, by then registered to work in the U.S. as foreign nationals, would vote in their native countries by absentee ballot or by traveling back to vote. They would pay taxes in the U.S. and would be eligible for certain benefits and services as Congress may decide. Newer arriving illegals would have to be sent back and those legally here would have to have tamper-proof IDs – a considerable technical challenge. Companies that continued to employ illegals would be severely fined – something that hasn't happened yet. Illegals who have committed felonies should not be eligible for guestworker status.

The next step is to reform legal immigration and to do something about those who overstay visas. The latter will require a considerable system of investigators, lawyers, clerks, judges, and perhaps detention centers. The former simply requires a Congress with the will to do something on immigration that approaches common sense.

Britain, Canada and Australia have recently rewritten immigration laws to establish point systems whereby would-be immigrants are rewarded for job skills, education and English-language proficiency – the absolute opposite of the present American system, which rewards low job skills, illegal entry and low education levels. The numbers of legal immigrants should be reduced if we are to have a breathing spell comparable to the one we enjoyed from the 1920s to the 1970s. Cutting legal immigration in half, largely by dropping much of the family reunification numbers, would be a good start. If the U.S. took in half a million immigrants a year it would still exceed by far the generosity of any other nation. There should be a reordering of where people come from, too. Eastern Europe has been discriminated against since 1924, yet those immigrants are the easiest to absorb through intermarriage. By only the second generation, racial and language problems are erased. Obviously, the door should be opened to Eastern Europe, where millions are eager to emigrate to the U.S. – that was the intention of the Kennedy bill in 1965. Having a "global" band of about 20%, or 100,000 a year is a good idea, too. We should be bringing in the best and brightest from around the world, not the peasants of Central America. There should be more balance between East Asians and West Asians. Congress will have to sort this out. It is also vital to reduce red tape and delays in processing legal immigrants and granting naturalization papers. At present, those who take the legal route are penalized in numerous ways, including long delays. As with the other "death wish" issues in this book, strong Congressional action is needed to solve the problem in the best interests of the United States and its citizens. Congress and four presidents in a row have been dismal on this issue. No one asked the American people if they wanted an India-sized population or an eventual Hispanic majority. Congress, through its inaction and some specific actions, has brought this crisis about. It has amounted to a kind of insanity – a perfect example of the philanthropy/ permissiveness approach misapplied to a serious national issue. A good example of this mode of thinking has been the declaration by some 80 communities (including libertarian San Francisco) that they are "sanctuary cities," which will not obey federal laws on the issue. Such outlaw communities should have all federal programs cut until they comply with the law. But when the president himself refuses to obey the laws he has sworn to uphold, there is obviously a precedent for lawlessness.

Congressional incumbency has been a problem in dealing with the immigration problem, as it has with other issues. In the U.S. Senate a clubby atmosphere developed on this issue among long-serving senators, including Republican senators who should have known better: John McCain, Lindsey Graham, Arlen Specter, Orrin Hatch, Trent Lott and others, including, outside the Senate, the entire Bush family. They have failed the American people on immigration. They are a collective argument for term limits and age limits. Graham, it should be noted, has taken a strong stand in favor of amending the Constitution in order to prevent Mexicans and others from coming to America specifically to have their babies here – "anchor babies." That is welcome, but his overall record on the larger issue is a poor one.

The Obama administration is even worse than these country club Republicans. As noted, he is a proponent of the phony and disastrous "comprehensive" immigration reform previously pushed by pro-Mexico, pro-cheap labor Republicans. In short, he is dedicated to making things even worse than they are – because he sees a political dividend in doing so.

Current immigration policy undermines the two-party system, creates an enormous new class of people dependent on government (due to welfare and food stamp dependency, runaway birth rates, poverty), bankrupts our state governments, increases crime, creates alienation and divisions, splits the nation linguistically, and promotes to power the political party that expands government activities and costs and makes the nation weaker in many ways, including in its military posture.

The goals should be to end the invasion, reorder immigration in America's best interests and to promote assimilation. Every effort should be made to have a breathing spell from mass immigration, whether legal or illegal, and to assimilate the newcomers as successfully as the last great immigration wave was assimilated in the decades from the 1920s to the 1970s.

There are five billion poor people in the world; obviously, they can't all come to America – rather, the American example must be attempted where they live. We can't even take in the unhappy half of Mexico's population without permanently altering our nation in ways unacceptable to most of us. Reform of immigration, legal and illegal, has been lacking for three decades because of poor leadership in the White House and in Congress.

THE THIRD CHALLENGE:
JUDICIAL ACTIVISM

What almost no one in America today seems to realize is how small the Founding Fathers envisioned the impact of the Constitution to be on daily life. Their 1789 federal constitution was meant to be extremely limited in its overall application. It was not intended to become what it is today – a tool for scrutinizing every aspect of American life and every rule, requirement, Congressional or legislative statute, and every imaginable behavior for its "constitutionality." This insanely broad application of the Constitution to nearly everything going on in America is a result of the vigorous "judicial activism" of recent decades – an activism that has been unreflectively accepted by the people, the media and politicians, despite that it actually has no constitutional basis. Amazing as it may seem, there is no warrant for judicial activism in the 1789 Constitution. Read Article Three of the Constitution, which deals with the courts, and you will see that this is so.

The Constitution, though revered, had plenty of flaws. The procedures to follow when electing a president or when a president dies in office or dies before taking office but after being elected, was so ill-considered that it has required three additional constitutional amendments to clarify the issues – plus a fourth one to apply term limits to the presidency.

A much more glaring error was the failure of the members of the Constitutional Convention (in Philadelphia, 1787) to consider what would happen if Congress or someone else deliberately violated the Constitution's provisions. For example, if Congress passed a law increasing the term of office for House members from two years to four, that would be a clear violation of the Constitution. Who would declare it so? And who would enforce the ruling of unconstitutionality? The Constitution is silent on these issues. In fact, the article describing the federal courts and their duties is by far the smallest of the three articles describing the principal branches of government. Congress is first, with the longest entry; the president is second; the courts are third and least.

This is not an accident. Supporters of the Constitution, including James Madison, "the Father of the Constitution" and the prime mover at the convention, published articles in key New York newspapers to persuade New York to ratify the new constitution. These articles, published between Oct. 27, 1787, and May 28, 1788 (date of publication, in book form, of the last papers, numbers 78-85), became collectively known as "The Federalist Papers," and later were published together, in two volumes, as *The Federalist*. Adoption of the new constitution required approval from nine of the original thirteen states, under the rules for passing legislation of the previous constitution, known in history as the Articles of Confederation. Approval by nine states was also in keeping with Article Seven of the new constitution.

The authors of *The Federalist*, an enduring classic, were

Madison, John Jay and the brilliant Alexander Hamilton –
who, in Federalist Paper #78, made a case for judicial review
– the notion that the courts should have the authority to
determine constitutionality, calling the judges, "the guardians
of the Constitution." However, Federalist Paper #78 was
published *after* eight states had already ratified and just before
two more (Virginia and New Hampshire) did. Consequently,
New York's acceptance was not decisive, though much
sought, when it came late in July by the close vote of 30-27,
with the understanding that a Bill of Rights would be soon
added (it was proposed the next year and adopted the year
after that, 1790).

It is important to point out that Federalist Paper #78 is
not part of the Constitution and had little to do with the
ratification by ten states prior to New York's ratification. The
idea is taken up again by Hamilton in his Federalist Paper
#81, but less vigorously. Hamilton outlines a view that was
modestly present among convention members and never
articulated in the Constitution itself: a right of the courts "to
pronounce legislative acts void," with the concomitant idea
that "The interpretation of the laws is the proper and peculiar
province of the courts." He added the sensible idea that "the
Constitution ought to be preferred to the statute" if there was
"an irreconcilable variance between the two…"

But Hamilton quickly adds that such an exercise of judicial
review (he calls it "judicial discretion") by the courts does
not "by any means suppose a superiority of the judicial to the
legislative power." He does say, though, that such judgments
operate as "a check" on legislative bodies, though only "with
a view to infractions of the Constitution only." The fanciful

rendering of judgments of "unconstitutionality" that occur with monotonous regularity today, in absurd and fanciful contexts (topless dancing, begging in the subways, unisex bathrooms) would have alarmed Hamilton. Like the other Founders he could not have imagined such a reckless misuse of judicial review.

Proof of this is in the same Federalist Paper #78, in which Hamilton quotes the French political philosopher, Baron de Montesquieu (who had advanced the idea of a three-part government – legislative, executive, judicial – in his famous 1754 study, *The Spirit of the Laws*), to the effect that the courts would be the weakest part of the federal government.

Hamilton wrote that in a government with separation of powers, "the judiciary, from the nature of its functions, will always be the least dangerous to the political rights of the Constitution; because it will be least in a capacity to injure or annoy them." A bit later, he added: "This simple view of the matter suggests…proves incontestably, that the judiciary is beyond comparison the weakest of the three departments of power…"

This does not sound like the judiciary we live with today!

Hamilton, in a footnote, then quotes Montesquieu himself, whose book was almost contemporary with those of the revolutionary and founding generation: "The celebrated Montesquieu, speaking of them, says: 'Of the three powers above mentioned, the judiciary is next to nothing.'" Hamilton then cites volume and page number of Montesquieu's book for that quotation. "Next to nothing" may have been what Montesquieu had in mind in *The Spirit of the Laws* and may be close to what James Madison intended when he adopted

Montesquieu's separation-of-powers model for the United States, but it is certainly not what we have today.

The awful and unconstitutional growth of judicial power as a possibility – a perversion of the judicial process – did not escape Hamilton. On the same page with the Montesquieu quote, Hamilton warned: "the general liberty of the people can never be endangered from that quarter…so long as the judiciary remains truly distinct from both the legislature and the Executive." He then adds that he agrees with Montesquieu that "'there is no liberty, if the powers of judging be not separated from the legislative and executive powers…'" (again quoting from *The Spirit of the Laws*). Hamilton then remarks, in his own words, "that as liberty has nothing to fear from the judiciary alone, but would have every thing to fear from its union with either of the other departments."

It should be noted that Hamilton was generally anti-democracy and thought of the general public as something of a mob, easily given over to depravity, as he put it. Thomas Jefferson, on the other hand, was much more enthusiastic about democracy, just then beginning to develop in America's frontier states. It is also obvious that Hamilton expected the courts to hew very closely to the Constitution when defending it. He would not have approved of the free-wheeling interpretations in modern times based on flexible phrasing such as "equal protection of the laws," "due process" or "establishment of religion." Hamilton did not intend the Constitution to become a Rorschach Test blob upon which the judges could see or read anything they wished.

What the members of the convention had really intended can be deduced from the fact that they specifically denied a veto over Congressional legislation by the courts, while granting one to the president. Furthermore, the president's veto is itself subject to reversal by Congress – with a two thirds vote of both bodies required. It stands to reason that had the convention granted a similar veto to the courts that they would have established a similar check and balance. On July 22, 1787, in convention, the judicial veto was voted down, with Nathaniel Gorham of Massachusetts pointing out that members of the court were not qualified by political experience to judge laws of Congress and that judges in England had no such veto. Another prominent delegate, Elbridge Gerry, also of Massachusetts, argued that such a judicial veto would be a violation of the separation of powers (which it certainly is) and most in the convention agreed with him. This was the second time the veto had been rejected. In the previous month, a motion to establish a presidential-judicial hybrid, a "Council of Revision," to pass judgment on Congressional laws, also was turned down.

The members of the Constitutional Convention refused to grant powers of impeachment to the courts (where, logically, it would seem appropriate) because the Supreme Court had too few members and such a small body was liable to bribery or other corruption. Consequently, the House would impeach and the U.S. Senate convict.

The founding generation, especially Madison, was strongly influenced by the great Sir William Blackstone, a celebrated Oxford law professor whose Commentaries on the Laws of England (a multivolume work) was contemporaneous with the American movement toward independence. Regarding judicial review in England, Blackstone had written that courts could not overturn a law of Parliament because that would put judicial authority over that of the legislative authority, which would obviously undermine the sovereignty of parliament. Such a pronouncement by Blackstone may explain why Madison did not overtly endorse judicial review at the convention. In fact, when arguing for his "Council of Revision," he made it clear that a presidential-court veto (from either or both), if adopted, could be overturned by a super majority in Congress.

In his recent study, *Packing the Courts: The Rise of Judicial Power and the Coming Crisis of the Supreme Court,* political scientist James MacGregor Burns, a lifelong student of the courts and of American politics, speaking of the members of the Constitutional Convention, clearly states that the Framers did not give the court a right to overthrow laws of Congress nor did they intend that the courts would hold sway over the other two branches of the federal government.

How, then, did we arrive at the extreme situation we suffer under today? Beginning with the horrendous Dred Scott decision in 1857, the federal courts have increasingly become a branch of the legislature – the unelected, absolutist branch. They have done this by misusing judicial review. It's a simple process: the judges, acting on a suit filed in federal court, overthrow some existing law, rule, regulation or requirement by declaring it unconstitutional – whether it has anything to do with the Constitution or not. Unconstitutionality is the grab-all term that can apply to just about anything going on in America that someone, somewhere, doesn't like.

The judges do three things: first, with great solemnity and "landmark" pomp, they declare the offending law unconstitutional; second, they write a substitute law of their own; finally, they impose the substitute law on the entire nation – and they do so with the grace of a piano falling out of an apartment window. Unlike laws from Congress, legislatures, city or county councils or other bodies, a law from the courts has no flexibility and no time limit. It cannot be tweaked, amended or repealed. It is set in concrete forever. Yes, theoretically, it could be repealed by a constitutional amendment, but of over 4,000 constitutional amendments introduced in Congress since 1791, only 17 have been adopted (because of the difficulty of getting two thirds of both houses of Congress and three fourths of the states to ratify). Amendment is not really an option.

The other simple way a court-passed law could be overturned would be for a future court to reverse the judgment. This occasionally happens, but even when the future court is ideologically different from the original court, judges are reluctant to overturn precedent, which, as all lawyers know, is the foundation for all future action on the same issue. There is one other way to block the courts specified in the Constitution, but Congress, unfortunately, has shown no stomach for limiting appellate court jurisdiction on a case by case basis. Consequently, we are stuck with these unconstitutional laws which themselves amount to illegal constitutional amendments. This serves those (mostly liberals) who are in love with the notion of an "evolving Constitution" – that is, one that can mean anything the judges want it to mean, as activist Justice William Brennan often put it.

In this illegal fashion the courts can amend the Constitution hundreds of time, while Congress and the public can almost never amend it. All the activists need is five votes on the Supreme Court. By 5-4 votes, they can effect massive social and political changes. Something (like sodomy) can be unconstitutional one decade by a 5-4 vote, then be constitutional by a similar vote a few years later (after a president has replaced a retiring judge). Hence the intense politicizing of the bench, beginning with the nominating process.

If even Hamilton, one of the few supporters of judicial review at the time, was convinced the court would be by far the weakest branch of government and would never have any legislative powers, how did we get to situation today in which it is the strongest branch? The answer is that the Supreme Court itself, out of whole cloth, created its absolute right of judicial review. The case was *Marbury v. Madison* (1803), a landmark case if there ever was one. In 1801, a Federalist Party appointee named Marbury was one of many "midnight" appointments made by the outgoing Federalist administration of John Adams. The new president, elected in 1800, was a Republican, Thomas Jefferson – and, since Marbury's papers were not delivered in time, Jefferson refused his appointment as a justice of the peace in the District of Columbia. Marbury sued for his job in federal court and John Marshall, who had been for a short time Chief Justice (and a strong Federalist) ruled with his majority that Marbury deserved to be approved for the job (thus insulting Jefferson's judgment on the matter), but that, technically, he couldn't be approved because the section of the Judiciary Act of 1789, passed by Congress, had wrongly interpreted the court's jurisdictional rights because these were in conflict with Article III of the

Constitution, which spelled out the jurisdiction of the courts. Thus Marshall had it both ways – his court overthrew a law of Congress but also kept Marbury from being seated in his new job – which pleased the Jeffersonians and kept them from retaliating politically. On the surface, Jefferson had won, but beneath the surface a terrible precedent had been set – one not appreciated fully at the time. It would be 54 years before another law of Congress would be overthrown by the courts, but state laws and state court rulings would be overturned by the Marshall Court long before that.

The next landmark Congressional court decision based on "constitutionality" was the Dred Scott Decision in 1857, probably the worst decision ever made by the Supreme Court. It overruled the massive Congressional compromises over the extension of slavery worked out in Congress in 1820 and 1850. This misjudgment by the court led directly to the Civil War, in which more than half a million Americans died and entire cities were devastated.

This misuse of judicial review has come to be known as judicial activism – and it can cut both ways. From the post-Civil War period into the late 1930s, the court's activism favored business and property interests at the expense of the public interest. Again and again, Congressional and state laws and other statutes were struck down because they were opposed by big corporations, banks and business interests of the time. Such laws included those protecting women and children in the workplace, wages and hours regulations, rights of labor unions and other progressive measures taken for granted today. This "conservative activism" climaxed in the mid 1930s with a flurry of decisions overruling key Congressional laws that made up the structure of Franklin Roosevelt's New Deal. Roosevelt was so angry that he proposed enlarging the court from nine to thirteen members, which would give him enough appointments to arrange a new, friendlier majority. This "court-packing" tactic was badly handled by FDR and it backfired politically. But the conservative court almost immediately reversed direction by approving the Wagner Act (rights of labor unions to collective bargaining) and some other liberal measures. Within a few years attrition gave FDR the appointments he needed and World War II distracted almost everyone from the New Deal. In the 1940s the court took a decidedly liberal turn, much expanded in the 1950s under the leadership of Chief Justice Earl Warren, the most activist Chief Justice in history.

On the last page of his book, *Packing the Courts*, Professor Burns declares boldly that the Marshall court was mistaken and that *Marbury v. Madison* has been stretched beyond reason to serve special interests. Burns is right, of course, but he is upset by the misuse of judicial review by conservative judges. About misuse by liberals, a hallmark of our time, he has little to say, presumably because he agrees with *Roe v. Wade* and similar decisions.

This author finds the earlier conservative activist decisions, beginning with Dred Scott, to be appalling, but finds equally appalling the left-libertarian activist decisions of the past half century or so: decisions on religion in the public place, abortion, pornography, and the like. Burns sees conservative activism operating today in recent court decisions on gun ownership, school busing, affirmative action, campaign financing, separation of church and state, partial birth abortions, and, especially, *Bush v. Gore*, the decision in 2000 that more or less decided the presidential election (though later recounts and surveys showed Bush would have won, anyway).

Burns is right on some of these counts. An outrageous conservative-activist decision recently was *Kelo v. City of New London*, in which the Supreme Court expanded the traditional application of eminent domain (seizure of your personal property – including land or even your house, at "just compensation," for public use, as specified in the Fifth Amendment). The court effectively expanded it to include future commercial or private development that might be good for the community, hence an interpretation of "public use" that stretches and expands the term. Clearly, this could lead to wholesale appropriation of private property on behalf of business or commercial interests. It was a bad decision, although voted by a 5-4 majority, as most of these more recent conservative decisions have been. One liberal judge replacing a moderate or conservative, could undo all these "conservative" decisions, including the recent one against certain Chicago gun ownership restrictions.

Most Americans, judging by polls and surveys since 1963, are much more upset about liberal-activist decisions – the ones that gave us abortion on demand, the banning of prayers and religious displays in schools and other public places, and the extraordinary explosion of pornography in the 1970s and after.

Roe v. Wade is the best example of liberal-activism run amok. Early in 1973 the Supreme Court discovered a fundamental, constitutional right to abortion that had somehow escaped nearly everyone's attention for 184 years. The decision was based on the discovery of a "right to privacy" in *Griswold v. Connecticut,* a case in 1965 that established a right to birth control, contra some state laws, by citing a "right to privacy" lurking in the First, Third, Fourth, Fifth and Ninth Amendments. No one had been bright enough to see this before.

Granted that many laws on sexual behavior have been foolish and continue to be foolish in states where they still exist – but the words "right to privacy" are nowhere in the Constitution. The Third Amendment forbids quartering troops in your home without your consent during peacetime; and the Fourth Amendment requires a properly certified search warrant before authorities can enter your home. There is a definite sense of a right to privacy expressed in these amendments but stretching them to include use of birth control or a right to abortion, is a bridge too far. The use of loose and general phrasing is a hallmark of court activist behavior. Justice William O. Douglas, another prominent liberal activist, went so far as to use the word "penumbra" (a shadowy presence) to suggest that certain rights lurked or were hidden, like raisins in a pudding, in the more general wording of the Constitution and its amendments. With such an imaginative approach, just about anything can be read into the Constitution. It strongly suggests that there is no area of life that the judges will not intrude into if some disgruntled individual or group files suit about the issue, however arcane. Another example of such an imaginative approach was the recent one-judge decision in California in which a gay judge, Vaughn Walker, overthrew a state constitutional amendment against gay marriage (approved by seven million voters) on Fourteenth Amendment grounds, freely misinterpreting and falsely applying "due process" and "equal protection of the laws" phrasing meant originally to apply to ex-slaves only. The plain fact is that neither marriage nor abortion is a genuine constitutional issue.

There is one way abortion rights *could be* constitutional and that is by adopting a constitutional amendment, but this hasn't happened. Also, any state could pass its own version of *Roe v. Wade*, and ultimately, Congress could pass a national *Roe v. Wade* law. But, as with so many critical issues, including gay marriage or civil unions, Congress has ducked the problem and left it up to the courts. In Britain, Parliament was brave enough to pass a national civil union statute and that solved the problem in typical British pragmatic fashion. These weighty issues should be decided by democratic consensus and it is interesting that just lately (2011) some polls, including Gallup, showed a slight majority favoring, for the first time, acceptance of same-sex marriage in the United States.

In the 1960s there was a considerable increase in illegal abortions (because they were criminalized in most localities, though available on request in New York and a few other states). Oddly, this increase occurred in tandem with the invention and broad distribution of the most effective birth control technology in human history – the oral contraceptive pill, largely the work of American biologist, Dr. Gregory Pincus, and his research team. Despite availability of "the pill," abortions were increasing, largely because abortions were being used as birth control. There are wildly different opinions as to the numbers, but the totals for the early years after *Roe v. Wade* may give an indication that illegal abortions may have been in the neighborhood of 300,000 a year and rising. Obviously there was a problem.

After *Roe v. Wade*, illegal abortions dropped dramatically, as can be readily understood. But legal abortions began to skyrocket – far beyond the 300,000 to 400,000 that may have occurred previously when abortion was illegal. By the late '70s abortions had reached 1.2 million a year (or about one in three or four conceptions) and abortion numbers peaked in the late '80s at about 1.3 million a year. In recent years, despite a rapid growth in overall population, the number of abortions and the rate of abortions have dropped significantly. It is difficult to make a moral case for the use of abortion as birth control, but in the '70s that was the situation for most abortions. The majority of abortions were for young, unmarried women who admitted they did not use birth control. This enormous increase in abortions sparked a debate that is still vigorous today.

What reformers were trying to do was to accept the fact that illegal abortions had reached high numbers and to allow them to be medically clean and safe so that injuries or deaths to the mothers could be prevented. Deaths and injuries were relatively rare, but "back alley" abortions were notorious for their risks. Justice Harry Blackmun and others on the Supreme Court who were sympathetic to women seeking abortions did not intend a huge increase in abortions. Their law regulating abortion was mindful of the value of human life and set limitations on abortions in the second and third trimesters of pregnancy. Obviously, human life is the highest value in the law and in common experience, and no one on the court sought a runaway growth in abortions – though that is what happened. Regardless of what the court intended in their 7-2 vote, they unleashed a tidal wave of legal abortions that grew year to year for several years and now numbers, in total, some 50 million. Any society that kills 50 million children in their mothers' wombs is not altogether either moral or civilized. Had Americans muddled through the issue in democratic fashion, in Congress and/or at the state legislature level, the death toll would surely have been much lower. What is undeniable is that when legal abortions are restricted, illegal ones rise and at a certain point the two lines cross with no cessation of abortions overall. Nevertheless, this was a prime example of Congress once again flunking a major issue and ducking its responsibilities – more than happy to let the courts carry the burden.

The justices in the *Roe* majority had established the principle that an American woman had a legal, constitutionally protected right to abortion under most circumstances. These circumstances were broadened in later court decisions refining *Roe v. Wade*. The problem is that there is not a shred of constitutional legal basis for such a ruling. It is a perfect example of philanthropy/permissiveness from the upper class toward everyone else: Do as you please, we don't care. Polls at the time showed a majority in disagreement with *Roe*, and over the decades since then a solid majority for the permissive *Roe* standard has never developed, though in recent years surveys show a majority approving legalized abortion. On the other hand, a recent poll indicated that most Americans consider abortion to be murder. It seems the public has decided that abortions should be legal but somewhat restricted – in other words, not on-demand. In this they reject the previous criminalization of abortion but do not accept the on-demand argument of *Roe*. If left to the states, there would obviously be many restrictions on abortion, but some states (Nevada, California, New York) would likely have *Roe* standards – but many others (Minnesota, the Dakotas, Louisiana, Utah, perhaps Texas) would not.

Abortion has slowed the growth of the white American population and is now doing the same to the black population. In the 1960s, the esteemed black novelist and essayist, James Baldwin, defended black welfare dependency by saying that at least blacks didn't kill their children through abortion, as whites did. He would be appalled today to learn that the black abortion rate is now higher than the white rate, which has declined in recent years. Abortion rates are low among Asians and Hispanics, the fastest growing populations in America.

The same judicial permissiveness permeated decisions on pornography, which increasingly came under First Amendment free speech protection in a series of court decisions in the '60s and '70s. The Mafia and others who produced porno films in California bankrolled legal challenges to anti-porn statutes in states and communities. Most of these local governments could not afford the legal fees to fight all the way to the Supreme Court, so they gave in. Eventually, Cincinnati and Omaha were among the very few large cities where porn shops were not allowed within city limits. The cultural influences of porn, beginning about 1971 with the first public displays, have not yet been seriously assessed, but they may be profound. As noted, it is one thing for such cultural/moral changes to come about because of changing public tastes or attitudes – in other words, from the people up. It is another thing for such changes to be driven from the top down, by elites imposing their own permissive culture on everyone else.

Besides abortion, the court issue that has been most controversial is separation of church and state. If anything, the public was in stronger disagreement (and remains so) with anti-religion decisions than with abortion decisions.

Beginning in the early 1960s the courts have made a series of rulings that amount to a war on religion – and that religion is Christianity. What almost no one, including those in the press and media, seem to understand is how radical this trend by the courts has been. The 1787 Constitution, as any American history teacher knows, has only two prohibitions on religion: There shall be no religious test for holding public office and the Congress shall not establish an official, tax-supported state church. Both of these restrictions reflected the situation in England at the time. For several centuries, membership in the Church of England (formalized by Queen Elizabeth in the 16th century), was required by those holding public office. Non-members could be persecuted, imprisoned and even executed. For centuries, non-members of the "established" Church of England suffered discrimination. This drove some of them (Puritans and Pilgrims) to emigrate to Holland, America and other places. Article Six of the U.S. Constitution makes it clear that there may be "no religious test" for holding federal office at any level.

The First Amendment to the Constitution was also meant to be clear: There will be no established church. Madison, who wrote the Amendment and presented it to Congress, said that there were too many Christian denominations in the states and none of them had a majority, nationally. Consequently, it would be unfair to choose one of them, including the U.S. version of the Church of England (the American Episcopal Church), over any of the others. However, it was perfectly legal for a state to have an "established," tax-supported church – and some of them did, continuing for decades after the adoption of the Federal Constitution. The largest denominations of the time included the Congregational Church, influential in New England and established in Massachusetts, the Episcopal Church (which had many elite members and was established in some states) and the Presbyterian Church.

Madison had to rewrite his amendment several times to avoid certain pitfalls. The original version stated that no national religion shall be established. That wording might have prevented today's authoritarian secularists from misinterpretating the final wording, "Congress shall make no law respecting an establishment of religion." The clear intent was to forestall the establishment of one Christian denomination as a state-supported church over all the others.

Madison changed his original wording because the word "national" irritated anti-Federalists (the people who coalesced, politically, around Jefferson in 1800) because they found the Constitution itself too "national," at the expense of the states. The congressional committee Madison was working with suggested this wording: "No religion shall be established by law." Madison was amenable to the wording as long as it was understood to mean that Congress would not establish a religion or enforce a legal observation of it.

Members from Connecticut did not agree because they feared such a wording would interfere with the normal exercise of religious practice (including that in Congress and the Federal Courts, where God was acknowledged and there was a Congressional chaplain). Madison then restored the word, "national," in order to clarify what he meant: that one Christian denomination, or a combination of denominations, would not become a tax-supported established church. But, again, the word "national" was too controversial, so Madison rewrote that portion of the First Amendment dealing with religion in the final form as we have it today: "Congress shall make no law respecting an establishment of religion, or prohibiting the free exercise thereof."

Madison had no intention, nor did Congress when they accepted the amendment, to build "a wall of separation" between church and state. That attitude was held by some, including Jefferson, who wrote the phrase in a letter, years later, to a group of Baptists. But it was not Madison's intent. Also, the amendment was binding only on *Congress,* meaning the federal government. It did not apply to the states, which could each have an established religion if they so chose – as some of them had.

For centuries American school children decorated their public school classrooms for Christmas and sang Christmas carols in class and at school assemblies. Public prayer at graduation ceremonies and other school events was taken for granted and was an integral part of the culture. Standard grade school reading texts were full of biblical stories and lessons and the Ten Commandments was prominently displayed, not only in classrooms but in other public places.

The war on religion which has been waged by the courts since the early 1960s does not represent any movement on the part of the American people, nor does it accurately reflect the Constitution. It has been an exercise in elitist, authoritarian secularism running roughshod over Congress, the states and the people.

Not that there is anything inherently wrong with a strict separation of church and state. Some countries have it and seem to get along fine. But our country is not one of them. As with abortion, if this issue were left to Congress and the states, most prohibitions against the recognition of religion in public places would not exist. Some school districts where non-Christian students predominate, or where left-liberal sentiments are in the majority, might have separation statutes. That would be a normal exercise of democracy at the local level and an expression of majority rule within that district or county or city. But the vast majority of Americans have professed Christianity since the first English landing at Jamestown in 1607 and prayers in school and other public places were the norm, not the exception.

In almost every nation and empire that has ever existed the state recognizes the majority religion with special favor. This is true whether the religion is Islam, Buddhism, Hinduism, paganism or Christianity. "Civic religion" is the frank admission by the state that the majority religion is a vital part of the nation's culture and a support to civilization and good behavior. America was like nearly all other societies in history – the state recognized the importance, the high place, of the majority religion – while also tolerating other religions.

How, then, have we reached the point where religion in schools and public offices is considered dangerous and subversive – something to be stamped out?

The American intelligentsia had become less and less religious, in traditional terms, in the second half of the 20th century. Religion is not intellectually fashionable, unless in the personal development, New Age mode.

A permissive elite does not take kindly to the rather restrictive demands of traditional Christianity, especially in areas of personal conduct. It took a long time for these elite attitudes, intellectual and artistic, to permeate Hollywood films, TV programs, popular music and the Broadway stage, but by the 1960s the trend was unmistakable. Hollywood dropped its production code in the 1960s and almost immediately, R-rated movies began to crowd out other movies. Nudity, profanity, sadistic violence and simulated sex became the norm. For decades now, a majority of Hollywood movies have been rated R or PG-13 (today as rough as R movies were in the '60s), despite the fact that G-rated and PG movies do much better at the box office. Television held out longer, but unregulated cable TV entertainment has joined movies at the same level of disinterest in traditional religious norms and reflects the same resentment of traditional Christianity (with the Mormon faith singled out for particularly vicious hits). The permissive side of philanthropy/permissiveness dominates in popular entertainment.

Literary fiction continued a pessimism that went back to the late 19th century and was accelerated after the horrors of the First World War, and even the newer Broadway musicals became dark, pessimistic and bereft of religious redemption or fulfillment. High art, also, took a turn toward the ugly and sensational (novelty above skill, as Tom Wolfe pointed out so deftly, and with stinging humor, in his *The Painted Word*). The culture of the upper classes was definitely lacking transcendental religious thinking, unless of the personal improvement, New Age variety. The movies and plays of the '70s, perhaps reflecting the Vietnam War era, were relentlessly dark and doom-laden, often with the hero killed at the end or with the hero an anti-hero as bad as the villains he faced.

The optimism, respect for religion, and generally upbeat nature of most Hollywood movies of the past, had disappeared (though there had always been some tragic films and violent films, going back to the silent era). Musicals, the happiest of family movies, vanished in this era of new realism.

Polls show only about 20% of Americans defining themselves as "liberal," with over 40% defining themselves as conservative. Yet the elite in America are overwhelmingly liberal. Surveys of some 800 Eastern media reporters and editors found them to be about 80% liberal in outlook and Democrat in voting habits; polls of college professors provide similar results, as do surveys of NEA membership representing grade school and high school teachers. A survey showed that 80% of those working in the publishing industry voted for Barack Obama. Hollywood and the New York arts/entertainment community are likewise liberal by a large majority, as are the nation's librarians, if their national convention activities are any measure. Nearly all of the TV news networks (NBC, ABC, MSNBC, CNN, and CBS) are liberal. Fox News on cable is the sole exception. The nation's big city newspapers, especially the New York *Times*, but also the Boston *Globe*, Los Angeles *Times*, and the Washington *Post*, are predominantly liberal on their editorial pages and in recent years the New York *Times* has politicized its news columns and front pages, too.

Members of the judiciary seemed to share the new liberal/libertarian outlook, with its trend toward secularism and individualism, and began to treat religion as something subversive and dangerous to the public. The activity of the courts was a perfect exercise in philanthropy/permissiveness as it offered a philanthropic rescue of minority viewpoints while knocking down traditional Christian ones, in keeping with the new permissiveness in popular entertainment that also permeated the '60s/'70s culture.

The key decisions were *Engel v. Vitale*, in 1962 – in which daily prayers in a New York public school were declared unconstitutional, and *Murray v. Curlett* (1963) the case in which the well known, self-publicized atheist, Madalyn Murray O'Hair, sued to prevent one of her sons from the affront of hearing Bible readings at his Maryland school. The Murray case was consolidated with *Abington School District v. Schempp* (Schempp was a Unitarian who resented school Bible readings). The Supreme Court ruled in favor of the aggrieved minorities and against the vast majority of Americans (as expressed in surveys at the time and later). As in *Roe*, the subject of the original *Murray* case, William Murray, later disavowed the case, became an evangelical Christian and traveled about denouncing the court's decision. The real Jane Roe, Norma McCorvey, who had falsely claimed she was raped to get around Texas state abortion restrictions, followed the same pattern as William Murray

– religious conversion and activist rejection of her case and its decision. O'Hair, herself, was later murdered, along with members of her family, by a disgruntled employee. She had founded an institute for atheism, complete with published materials – hence it was one ideological sect against another (minority atheism vs. majority Christianity) and the courts chose atheism – ostensibly on the higher issue of religious "establishment," but in fact on the obvious platform of imposing their own secularism on the general public.

In each of the religious cases, the "establishment" clause of the First Amendment was cited as the authority. Oddly, in each case, the "free exercise" clause of the same amendment was actually being violated by the courts, in the view of many, including dissenting justices. Much of this anti-religious movement in the courts was derived from the application of the Fourteenth Amendment to the states by twining it with the First Amendment. Congress, by passing the Fourteenth Amendment just after the Civil War, was attempting to guarantee "equal protection of the laws" and "due process" for the newly freed black slaves. Congress proposed in the amendment that the ex-slaves, having been born in the United States (the slave trade had been cut off almost sixty years earlier, so nearly all slaves had been born here) were citizens and could not be deprived of "life, liberty or property" or of the "privileges and immunities" enjoyed by all other citizens. Interestingly, the Congress, in writing the Fourteenth Amendment did not specifically apply the amendment to the Bill of Rights, amendment by amendment. That happened later, over time, in various court cases, as each of the first eight amendments of the Bill of Rights was "incorporated" into the Fourteenth Amendment. In a great irony, a court case in 1940, *Cantwell v. Connecticut,* incorporated the "free exercise" clause of the First Amendment into the Fourteenth (in defense of Jehovah's Witnesses, who were proselytizing door to door), almost exactly the opposite of what happened 22 years later in *Engle v. Vitale,* when the "establishment" clause was used to interfere with religious freedom. It is very unlikely that the framers of the Fourteenth Amendment realized that the religious restrictions of the First Amendment would be applied to the states as a result of their new amendment.

The Fourteenth Amendment, because of its very general and loose phrasing, is given to widespread abuse by courts using the generality of the language to apply it to almost anything that strikes their fancy. The deliberate abuse of the establishment clause by judges who surely knew better merited impeachment, but Congress, despite a loud public outcry, lacked the courage to discipline the judges – and it still lacks that courage today.

Crucial to the entire issue, though, is the obvious fact that even if the First and Fourteenth Amendments are incorporated, the only restrictions on state religious policies would be the same as those on federal policy: no "established" church and no religious test for public office. Since the last established church at the state level, that in Massachusetts, was disestablished in 1833 and no states have a religious test for public office, there should be no other restrictions – no restrictions on prayer, Bible readings, Christmas carols, crèches, Menorah displays, Buddhist statues or any other religious manifestations in public places, schools or institutions at the state or local level. In fact, these practices, if they were allowed, would clearly come under the "free exercise thereof" clause in the First Amendment. To put it another way, the anti-religious decisions of the courts, which have been piling up since 1962, are all violations of the free exercise of religion guaranteed by the First Amendment and applied to the states under the Fourteenth Amendment.

That lawyers and judges have been extra clever in devising "penumbras" and other inventive rationalizations for their high-handed actions does not make their actions constitutional or even legal. Such decisions are becoming increasingly absurd, as in a recent ruling by a federal judge in Wisconsin that the National Day of Prayer, a Congressionally endorsed institution since 1952, is unconstitutional.

High handed behavior by federal judges is now the norm. A federal district judge in Missouri, Russell Clark, took over the Kansas City public school system and even demanded a tax on suburbanites to pour over $2 billion into the failing system. He should have been impeached and removed from office, but wasn't. As usual, Congress remained in paralysis. The Kansas City experiment didn't work, despite all the money spent (some of it on swimming pools and athletic equipment). Student scores did not improve, white flight continued, and many of those schools are now closed or closing. More recently, in Port Chester, New York, a town of 30,000 that is half "Hispanic," a federal judge, Stephen Robinson, demanded that voters adopt "cumulative voting" (each voter given six votes to apply to any of the candidates for Village Trustee). The idea was that this would result in the election of at least one Hispanic, and it did. This judge is another good candidate for impeachment and removal –

apparently it never occurred to him that all residents of the community are Americans and that there is no constitutional requirement for so many blacks, so many whites, so many Hispanics, in government, sports, entertainment or any other activity.

Members of the Supreme Court and all the other federal judges have no specific mandate to declare anything "constitutional" or "unconstitutional." In doing what they do they are enforcing an elitist culture on the rest of the population, using the philanthropy/permissiveness model. They exercise philanthropy by rescuing atheists, pornographers, abortionists and others who lack public approval from the overbearing majority rule that used to prevail. They invariably put the demands of aggrieved individuals or small groups ahead of majority interests and norms. State and county judges are now emulating the bad behavior of federal judges with similar rulings (including one in Florida striking down a ban on certain kinds of low-riding pants as a violation of the Fourteenth Amendment!). Human rights commissions, acting as ad hoc courts, can be just as foolish: Recently the Minnesota Human Rights Commission declared "ladies' nights" at bars to be illegal and discriminatory because women got cheaper drinks than men (that the men at the bars were more than willing to accept the situation seems to have escaped the self-righteous busybodies on the commission).

One can't help but wonder if the enormous guilt about African-Americans that surfaced in the 1960s during the civil rights movement, doesn't have something to do with the knee-jerk defense of almost any minority or individual who feels put upon by the majority. As in immigration, the elites are so guilty about the plight of minorities that they are driven to overemphasize minority interests.

But, in terms of minorities, didn't this long round of judicial activism begin with the Warren Court's *Brown v. Board of Education* decision? Yes, this truly landmark decision in 1954, ending segregated schooling, was the first of the Warren court's activist "constitutional" decisions and probably the most important and decisive one in terms of social change. It was also quite rightly based on an application of the "equal protection of the laws" clause of the Fourteenth Amendment. Since that amendment was directly and unequivocally based on the desire of Congress to provide equality for ex-slaves and their children, *Brown* stands the test of constitutionality. Warren, a former Republican governor of California, had been appointed chief justice the year before and went on to oversee one of the most activist courts in history. Between 1963 and 1969 the Warren Court nullified 16 federal and 113 state and local statutes. Warren is a good example of the bad luck Republican presidents have had in choosing nominees with the hope they will be conservative on the bench. From Warren in the 1950s to David Souter in the 1980s, many Republican nominees have turned liberal activist with a vengeance.

Brown is a good example of the very occasional, necessary ruling of unconstitutionality in regard to a local law or regulation (as was *Miranda v. Arizona*, based on the Fifth and Sixth Amendments). Claiming free speech for pornographers or overturning the Texas state law forbidding flag-burning or other desecration of the flag on the same grounds, are not.

Rulings of unconstitutionality should be rare – and that would be the case if the Constitution were understood to be what the Founders wanted it to be – a very limited document.

The Ninth and Tenth Amendments to the Constitution make it clear just how small the footprint of the Constitution was intended to be. Nearly everything going on in America was beyond its purview – the exact opposite of today, when nearly everything going on in America is scrutinized for its "constitutionality." This is an absurd situation in which laws passed by Congress, the states and localities lose the true force of law – because they remain weak and tentative until "tested in the courts." All laws are fatally undermined in this way, with people who resent a law or regulation ready to challenge it in federal court. As a result, there has been a significant increase in federal court lawsuits, encouraged by judicial activism. In his *The Evolving Constitution* (1992), Jethro Lieberman, a professor at New York Law School, wrote that John Marshall established a level of judicial review stronger than in any other nation – and so it has become. The evolving expansion of judicial review to its free-wheeling use today drastically undercuts the Ninth and Tenth Amendments.

The Ninth Amendment, in its entirety, states: "The enumeration in the Constitution, of certain rights, shall not be construed to deny or disparage others retained by the people." The Tenth Amendment, in its entirety, reads: "The powers not delegated to the United States by the Constitution, nor prohibited by it to the States, are reserved to the States respectively, or to the people." The clear meaning of this is that the Constitution is quite restricted and that the vast majority of rights and powers belong to the people and to their legislatures, city and county councils, and other forms of government. The people, exercising their judgment and freedom, are largely free of federal constitutional restrictions or controls. Only those powers specifically delegated to the Constitution are to be exercised by the federal government. Since very little is prohibited to the states, they should be more important and active than the federal government – and the people, in their myriad clubs, societies, businesses, schools, fraternal organizations, churches and neighborhood assemblies are largely free of federal government interference, according to the Framers. Judicial activism has stood the Ninth and Tenth Amendments on their heads, pushing federal intrusions into every corner of American life by encouraging federal lawsuits. Local government and self-government – so precious and necessary in a democracy – whether that of the Boy Scouts, the NCAA, the NFL, the state of Idaho, the city of Cincinnati, a borough, county, corporation, small business, local church, radio station, TV network, or one-man business, should not be threatened continually with federal lawsuits and judicial activism. Government should be healthy and effective at the local level and self-government even more so since it applies to nearly every organization in society.

What remedies are at hand for judicial activism? Nearly every good idea for reform has been floated earlier, going all the way back to the era of John Marshall. Stripping the courts of all right of judicial review, leaving us in the position of Britain or Switzerland, where parliamentary laws cannot be overturned by the courts, is one remedy – and it can be justified on the obvious grounds that the Constitution does not specifically grant a right of judicial review to the courts.

The problem with this approach is that we are accustomed to judicial review and it is apparent from notes and diaries of the members of the Constitutional Convention that they anticipated the court overthrowing laws directly contrary to the Constitution. As noted, Hamilton went even further, though still maintaining that the courts would be by far the weakest branch of the federal government.

The problem has not so much been judicial review itself, but the gross abuse of it by both conservative-activist judges and liberal-activist judges. Ideally, a federal judge would be non-activist – in other words, objective and respectful of the Constitution and its original meaning, but realizing there is elbow room for some interpretation and adjustment to changing times, without bending it absurdly backward as activist judges tend to do. Ironically, when just such a judge, Robert Bork, was nominated by President Ronald Reagan, he was unmercifully attacked and defamed by the Democratic majority on the Senate Judiciary Committee, the attack led by Sen. Ted Kennedy, whose vociferous smear of Bork was so over the top that it gave rise to the word, "Borking," as a description of political assassination. Kennedy claimed that Bork represented segregation, back alley abortions and censorship of writers and artists. Bork, who had a distinguished academic and circuit court background and had also been Solicitor General, favored restraint by judges, whom he felt should not legislate from the bench. He was not really a conservative activist so much as an originalist who didn't care for the freewheeling interpretations of activist judges. His one sin was a slightly eccentric support of states' rights in certain circumstances relating to voting rights. Because he was not an activist, he was ambushed by the committee, suffered character assassination, and was rejected in an effort led by Kennedy in one of his worst, foaming-at-the-mouth episodes in public life. Unlike the poorly prepared David Souter, Bork had a long paper trail – which is why, in recent years, presidents have gone for some nominees with little in the way of a record that can trip them up at confirmation hearings. The weirdest nomination of this sort was probably George W. Bush's nomination of Harriet Miers, his White House attorney and former staff secretary. She was close to the president and had a solid record as an attorney in private practice, but lacked the credentials one would expect in a Supreme Court nominee and was forced to withdraw after strong criticism from both sides of the political spectrum. Bush made up for this blunder by choosing two worthy conservatives, Chief Justice John Roberts and Samuel Alito, as his other nominees.

A remedy for activist abuse might be to pass a law of Congress that defines judicial review (this is the position of Burns). Congress could also require that a super majority of judges, say six or seven, be required for constitutional rulings. If seven of nine judges had to be in agreement, such rulings would occur less often – though some of the worst activist decisions have been made by large majorities. It would eliminate absurdities in which something is constitutional by a 5-4 vote one year and, by a similar vote, unconstitutional a few years later.

Another approach is to put judges up for election – so they would have to face the public. The Founding Fathers would be overwhelmingly opposed to this, for it would politicize the court and put it in the same boat as Congress. The public could elect a right-wing or left-wing Congress and president, with a court to match – not a good idea.

Should Congress have an easier method of replacing judges (other than the difficult impeachment process which requires votes in both Houses and a super majority in the Senate)? No, because that would politicize the court, too. One of the political parties, in solid control of Congress, could pack the court with new appointees.

Would increasing the number of judges make any difference? Probably not.

What about term limits or age limits? These are good ideas, but wouldn't have that much impact on judicial activism. The German Constitutional Court has 20-year appointments. A 25 or 30-year limit for our judges might be a good idea, as might be an age limit that is generous – say age 75 or 80.

Obviously, judicial review has been so abused by the courts that some kind of remedy must be sought or we will have unlimited judicial tyranny, which is incompatible with democracy.

As noted, one approach would be that of the British and many other parliamentary systems – simply strip the courts of judicial review. Another would be a check and balance on the courts. The latter is the better idea and the one adopted in Canada after that nation adopted a written constitution in the early 1980s. There is a mechanism for Parliament in Canada to defend its laws by overruling the Court if that body declares a law unconstitutional because it violates Canada's 1982 Charter of Rights and Freedoms (similar to our Bill of

Rights). But the procedure is complicated and involves using an "override power" that suspends judicial activism on the issue for five years – and is renewable. Provinces can use the same mechanism. So far, in the few cases that have arisen, Parliament has tended not to overrule the court. But Canada has suffered from an expansion of federal court activism, very much along the liberal-activist lines of U.S. court behavior, since adopting the Charter and a new constitution in 1982. But, unlike the United States, Canada does have some kind of check and balance.

Another approach would be an American-style checks and balances plan. Since the American Constitutional Convention specifically denied a veto power over Congressional legislation to the courts and now the courts regularly exercise just such a veto power, a Congressional check and balance, similar to the one on the president's veto, might be the best remedy for out of control judicial activism. A presidential veto can be overcome by a two-thirds vote in both houses of Congress. A three-fifths vote, easier to achieve, would be a proper discipline on the courts. The anti-religious decisions, or most of them, would likely have been overturned by Congress had this check been available at the time. This veto over the courts could extend to all decisions involving constitutionality, not just those in which Congressional laws are in question. The reform could even involve the president, for he could veto the Congressional response to the court, raising the bar to a higher super majority, for it would take a two thirds vote of both houses to overturn the president's veto. In this way, the president could side either with the court or with Congress, and all three branches of the government would have a say on constitutionality, though the court's initial move (perhaps with seven judges required) would carry the most weight, as it does in Canada.

A third approach would be a combination of the others. Taking the right of judicial review away from the courts for a ten year trial period would be an excellent remedy, but the political left would be hysterical about it, just as Ted Kennedy was hysterical when Robert Bork was nominated for the high court. An alternative would be to declare that the court's judicial review privilege is an advisory one, carrying no weight of law. In other words, the court would advise Congress or a state legislature or whomever the offending party is, that a statute, law or provision is unconstitutional in the court's majority view. The entity that had passed the offending rule or law would then have a set period of time to change or modify the law. If the deadline passes, the law remains and the court's advice on the issue is not taken. This process could involve Congress as a watchdog over the procedure, since Congress can overrule any law or statute by any lower legislature or organization. Getting something like this through Congress would not be easy, as liberals would fight to the death to stop it, given the fact that they strongly support the misuse of the courts as legislatures of last resort – legislatures that file diktats that override all other agencies and entities, both public and private.

Given the court's arrogance, there is a very real possibility that the federal courts might declare any reform of judicial activism, arriving as a Congressional law, to be unconstitutional. In that case, Congress and the states would have to pass a constitutional amendment to effect reform.

Even that might be contested as we have seen in California recently where a constitutional amendment, passed by the public, was challenged by the California Supreme Court for its "constitutionality." This is Alice in Wonderland stuff, but when elites seize power, they are reluctant to surrender it.

At present the courts have an unchecked power that is a clear danger to representative democracy and majority rule. Judges are appointed for life and have no term limits. A gaggle of bad judges, serving together for a long time and pushing a political agenda, can seriously undermine democracy. Most other democratic countries, including English-speaking ones, do not tolerate such a situation – and neither should we. Minority tyranny, in nearly every case, is bound to be worse than majority tyranny. The movement toward majority rule that began in England in 1688 is laudable and sensible. John Locke wrote, in his *Second Thesis of Government*, "…when any number of men have, by the consent of every individual, made a community, they have thereby made that community one body, with a power to act as one body, which is only by the will and determination of the majority…"

Putting a check and balance on the federal courts will require, as with the other three serious challenges, a strong and capable Congress, in touch with the public. With the exception of the Gingrich Congress of 1995-98, we haven't experienced much of that. Representative democracy must be preserved and protected by its representatives. Unfortunately, as with the other issues raised in this book and much more, the Congress remains dysfunctional.

THE FOURTH CHALLENGE:
A NEW AXIS OF DICTATORS AND THE
SPREAD OF NUCLEAR WEAPONS

The most ominous threat to human life and to the earth's environment is not global warming. It is nuclear war and the "nuclear winter" that would follow.

According to *Scientific American* magazine, in its January, 2010, issue, a regional nuclear war in which 100 atomic bombs are dropped would create a nuclear winter that would continue, with devastating effects on human, plant and animal life – and global climate – for up to ten years. The war theorized in the article is between India and Pakistan, two countries that gained nuclear weapons in the 1990s after several decades of domestic nuclear power development. Pakistan has recently tested ballistic missiles – the missiles that the United States and Soviet Russia developed half a century ago – which can carry nuclear explosives thousands of miles and land them on enemy cities with pinpoint accuracy.

The proliferation of nuclear weapons to India and Pakistan in the 1990s was the first step toward the perilous situation developing today, in which multiple nations, many of them dictatorships, are developing or have developed nuclear weapons and the missiles to deliver them far from their own territories (keeping in mind that they can also be delivered by ship, submarine, truck or airplane – suitcase bombs are a reality). If submarines from multiple countries fired nuclear-tipped rockets simultaneously at American targets, it would be nearly impossible to distinguish which countries owned the submarines. Bombs smuggled in across our porous borders or off-loaded at remote seacoast locations would also be difficult, if not impossible, to trace to their origins. Thus there is a very real possibility of a nuclear Pearl Harbor.

The United Nation's nuclear non-proliferation treaty (NPT) was established in 1968 and became binding on signatories in 1970. Some 187 nations (out of about 200 nation-states in the world) have signed the treaty, one of them being Iran. The treaty operates under the aegis of the International Atomic Energy Agency (IAEA), an oversight agency that serves as the inspection and enforcement branch of the UN. The treaty, and the thinking behind it, worked very well for half a century. From the 1940s, when the Anglo-American democracies and Soviet Russia developed nuclear weapons, until the 1990s, when India and Pakistan did, only three countries built them: France in 1960, China in 1964, and Israel in 1973. All three could offer sensible arguments for self defense and all three refrained from the insane level of nuclear bomb building that characterized Soviet behavior in the 1950s and '60s. The Soviets eventually had some 40,000 nuclear weapons, about twice the best estimates of the CIA, while the U.S. peaked at about 30,000. France and China kept their arsenals at a bare minimum for defense – about 300 apiece – while Israel has a smaller stockpile, estimated today at about 100 bombs. Keep in mind that 10 nuclear bombs would cripple a great nation like the United States and 100 would obliterate it. France, at the time it acquired the bomb, was facing a threat from the Soviets and was no longer a member of NATO – thus seeking an independent nuclear force under the leadership of President Charles De Gaulle, who distrusted the Anglo-Americans. China was facing the same Soviet threat, and Israel, with only a few million people, was surrounded by a large, hostile Arab community of some 100 million, with which it had already fought three wars (1948, 1956, 1967).

Of the nations with nuclear weapons during these decades only one, Russia, was a hostile and aggressive dictatorship. The Cold War was with Russia, organized then in a version of the old Russian empire known as the Soviet Union. The irrational hostility with which Russia then treated the West and China owed much to traditional Czarist insecurity and belligerence and much to Communist ideology. Attempts to explain Russia's behavior only in terms of Russian nationalism fail, as do explanations that stress Communism only. Both influences were operating in the minds of Soviet leaders who saw themselves as representatives of Greater Russia and its interests and as caretakers of Lenin's Marxist ideology, which operated as a secular religion, dominating education and the media within the Soviet state.

Consequently, only one hostile dictatorship had nuclear weapons for most of the Cold War (China keeping a low profile even after acquiring them) and there was only one opponent with which to play the dangerous nuclear chess game. Even so, the world came close to nuclear war several times, notably during the 1962 Cuban missile crisis.

The situation developing today is one in which multiple belligerent dictatorships will possess nuclear weapons and intercontinental missiles. The diplomatic situation is multipolar, rather than bipolar. Possibilities of disastrous mistakes are multiplied many times in such a situation. The relationships are inherently unstable, especially in regard to certain countries, like Venezuela and North Korea, where one emotionally or mentally ill individual may have all or most of the decision-making power.

That the great nations of the world are standing by while this potentially catastrophic situation has developed is mind-boggling. In the century just past, dictators directly caused the deaths of over 170 million people. The last Axis (Nazi Germany, Imperial Japan and Mussolini's Italy) started a war that killed some 60 million people. The chief victims were the aggressor nations and their prime targets of invasion. Japan lost two and a half million people while its principal victim, China, which it invaded in 1937, lost about ten million; Hitler Germany lost some seven million people while it's prime victim, the Soviet Union, which it invaded in 1941, lost a horrific 25 million soldiers and civilians.

You would think that Russia and China today would be in the forefront of nations seeking to forestall new wars. Japan, the only nation ever wounded by nuclear weapons, has sat by foolishly while North Korea, an economic midget, has built weapons that can destroy Japan, an economic giant. It is difficult to fathom this behavior – or that of South Korea, which has everything to lose, including its existence as a separate country.

Why would the great Western democracies, who suffered

so during World War II – Britain, the United States, France – and the new and very successful democracy in Germany – allow a new Axis to develop? As bad and as destructive as Hitler and the Japanese were during World War II, at least they did not have nuclear weapons. Hitler with the Bomb (and Tojo and Mussolini with the Bomb, too) is a prospect too horrible to contemplate. New York, London, San Francisco and Paris might have disappeared in mushroom clouds.

While members of the elite in Western countries are wringing their hands about global warming, which does not present as immediate a threat to human life and the environment as nuclear war and nuclear winter, the very real possibility of nuclear war becomes more likely every day. The behavior of dictators has taught us that they are sick, unstable personalities, given to rage, aggression and paranoia. Their willingness to kill – even to kill millions of people – has been well established. Dictators are rarely satisfied with absolute control of their own populations. Like Hitler and Mussolini and Stalin, they must expand their control beyond their borders by arming to intimidate or invade neighbors. A perfect example of this personality type is Hugo Chavez of Venezuela, a bumptious, ignorant, power-hungry individual who manipulated his way into power, then managed to get himself positioned to be president for life, and is now seeking the military power to project his ambitions beyond his borders (if he does not succumb to cancer first). A self-proclaimed Communist, fond of Lenin's authoritarian tract, *What Is To Be Done?*, Chavez has been a close ally of Fidel Castro and is bent on spreading leftist authoritarian systems in Latin America. Chavez promotes Communism despite the fact that it has collapsed everywhere as an economic system, most notably in China, where runaway economic growth has been achieved with modified capitalism and the junking of much of its state-sponsored Communist economic system. Chavez, with his overheated and over-excited rhetoric, paranoid sensibility, and unlimited appetite for power, is a perfect example of the kind of individual who should never have such power – and who certainly should never have a finger on a nuclear trigger. Yet three American presidents in a row have done nothing about his emerging dictatorship in Venezuela, in our backyard, within the sphere of the Monroe Doctrine. A terminal illness may provide the solution to Chavez's ambitions, but his remarkable success for many years is testimony to the paralysis in the United States engendered by political correctness and timidity.

The last three presidents have been equally ineffective in dealing with North Korea. It is obvious that the nations that have the most to lose if North Korea uses its nuclear bombs in anger – South Korea, Japan and China – have done little or nothing about the threat. South Korea, which has a decent conventional military, has fallen into something like the Stockholm Syndrome in relationship to its nasty neighbor. South Koreans riot over tainted beef imported from the U.S., Western free trade pacts, or over internal political issues, all the while ignoring a threat to their very existence. Not long ago South Korea suffered the insult of having one of its warships torpedoed by the North, killing 46 sailors. Not only was there little in the way of public protest, there was only a feeble response from the government. More recent aggression by North Korea has included the shelling of civilians – but, again, there has been little in the way of effective response from China, South Korea or Japan.

South Korea has twice as many people as North Korea (50 million to 25 million) and an economy 25 times larger. Yet South Korea did nothing to stop Kim Jong Il, the late dictator of North Korea, from building his nuclear weapons. The North is now building the missiles with which to deliver these bombs to Seattle, San Francisco and Los Angeles – while the U.S. remains as supine as South Korea. It is well to note that the Democratic party in the U.S. has consistently voted against funding for anti-missile systems, claiming as U.S. Senator Carl Levin of Michigan did once, that the U.S. can't afford them (in fact, their cost is minute within the bloated American federal budget). The real reason the Democrats oppose missile defense is an anti-military attitude – inspired by the war in Vietnam, a Democrat-instigated war. For Democrats, all wars are Vietnam, so we should prepare for none.

The president who made the most effective moves toward preventing nuclear weapons development in North Korea was Bill Clinton. Unfortunately, though Clinton did slow North Korea's course of action, and even stopped it for short periods of time, he was in the long run snookered by North Korea and his efforts failed. Clinton had an opportunity – at perhaps the prime moment to do so – to use a threat of force to stop the North's nuclear weapons program in the mid-nineties. Some of his advisors wanted him to do so, but he wouldn't. Instead he chose bribery as a method of stopping the North. The U.S. made an elaborate, much publicized deal with North Korea to supply fuel oil for the strapped North Korean economy, while the North Koreans made a pledge to not process plutonium or uranium – a pledge they didn't keep. Clinton's Secretary of State, Madeleine Albright, as noted, made a big show of visiting North Korea in 2000, Clinton's last year in office, to put a seal on the exchange, but the North Koreans admitted later they had no intention of keeping their part of the bargain.

Kim Jong Il did suspend his weapons development from time to time, both with Clinton and his successor, George W. Bush, probably because he genuinely feared military attack – which is what he, himself, would have ordered in a similar situation. The dictator was worried about an American military strike after Bush attacked Afghanistan in 2001 and Iraq in 2003, but, as it turned out, he had nothing to fear. Bush made an elaborate show of dropping Clinton's one-on-one diplomacy and replacing it with a six-sided diplomatic effort that brought Russia, China and other nations into the process – but this proved to be a waste of time. Practically speaking, Bush wasted *eight* years of precious time and it was on his watch that a working nuclear bomb device was successfully crafted in North Korea. As with the immigration crisis, Bush was less effective than Clinton.

Barrack Obama has pushed for sanctions against Iran to punish it for violating its NPT treaty obligations and has worked hard to engage Russia in the sanctions. In fact, Obama made a major concession to Russia by cancelling the not-yet deployed anti-missile system promised to Poland and the Czech Republic. The system was described by the Bush administration, which initiated it, as one against a future Iranian threat, but it was clearly aimed at Russia, which continues to maintain an enormous inventory of nuclear missiles aimed at Europe. Obama gave away his biggest negotiating card for rather nebulous promises by the Russians to help with Iranian sanctions. Later, in confusion, he resurrected some of the Polish participation, but moved most anti-missiles to ships. This has caused a row with Russia but falls far short of a robust system against either intermediate or (especially) intercontinental ballistic missiles. Only Bush II, of the past four presidents, pursued missile defense with purpose, and he fell far short of what Ronald Reagan had envisioned in his "Star Wars" recommendations.

In fact, neither Russia nor China will ever sign on to sanctions strong enough to slow, much less stop, Iran's nuclear weapons development. This should have been obvious to Obama since Russia has all along been the principal contributor to Iran's nuclear development. Obama, with his ivory tower attitudes and naïve foreign and defense policy assumptions, has been made to look foolish, very much as Clinton was made foolish by the North Koreans. Unilateral sanctions by Iranian trading partners other than Russia and China, are the only effective sanctions possible if the two dictatorships do not cooperate – but they have been very slow in coming. Sanctions against the Iranian central bank could stop Iran's economy in its tracks, as could interdiction of oil and gasoline shipments.

Iranian president Mahmoud Ahmadinejad has frequently threatened the destruction of Israel – and even of Britain and America. Recently an Iranian Ayatollah, head of the Hezbollah political faction in Iran, announced that Iran would conquer the Middle East and destroy Israel by creating a "Greater Iran," as a prelude to the return to earth of a legendary Shia Muslim messiah, the Mahdi. Obviously, securing nuclear weapons would be vital to such a project.

President Barack Obama's tendency to make a show of diplomacy in the face of such threats is typical . The UN made a great show of shuttling diplomats around in the 1990s during the Yugoslav crisis, drawing up position papers, making legal claims under international laws and treaties, staging long public deliberations and otherwise obfuscating while tens of thousands of innocent people in Bosnia and Croatia were slaughtered, often en masse, by Serb militias. Civilians flocked to UN-declared "safe havens," towns where small numbers of UN blue-helmeted forces promised sanctuary, only to learn to their horror that Serbs would brush aside the non-defending, lightly armed UN forces and round up their victims for slaughter. In recent years millions have also died in Africa, in tribal and political wars about which the UN was helpless and hapless.

Obama shares the left-liberal notion that it is the U.S. that is the cause of trouble in the world. Democrats since George McGovern have tended to see the Vietnam War (which they started and maintained) as typical of American aggression, hence the strange behavior of the Obama administration in apologizing for American behavior while kowtowing to Russia, Iran, Mexico, China and Middle Eastern countries at the beginning of Obama's presidency. Secretary of State Hillary Clinton even presented the Russian ambassador with a "re-set" gadget, to express our desire to start over, implying that the Bush administration had been too hard on Russia. In fact, Bush and his secretaries of state, Colin Powell and Condoleezza Rice, had gone all out to treat Russia with dignity, even to the point of overlooking its crimes (the attempted lethal poisoning of Ukrainian presidential candidate Viktor Yushchenko, the murders of various journalists and expatriates, and, near the end, the brutal invasion of Georgia). Bush invited Vladimir Putin, architect of Russia's bad behavior, to his ranch in Crawford, Texas, declaring that he had looked into Putin's eyes and seen his soul. Bush must need new glasses.

All of this derives from the unrealistic view that the world is a peaceful place and that we, as a San Francisco city council member put it, have little or no need of a military (this is the view of the "Occupy" movement, as well). Completely missing from the left-liberal outlook is any sense that the world is a dynamic place and that evil men are part of the dynamic. Contrary to the title of a popular book in the '90s, history has not ended. It goes on, boiling and pouring, with every possibility of repeating the invasions, wars, aggressions and disasters of the past, in which entire civilizations collapsed and disappeared and tens of millions of people perished.

Romans who had lived peacefully for generations in their towns, villas and farms in the regions near the Danube River in the fourth century AD, protected by imperial legions and endless military camps and forts along the river, had no idea that they would be attacked, pillaged, murdered, raped and enslaved by barbarian armies after their emperor made the foolish decision to allow two large German tribes to settle on the Roman side of the great river boundary. When the barbarians began to misbehave, that same emperor, with most of his best army, was slaughtered on a nearby battlefield. Seventy-five years later, the great Roman state, which had survived for some 800 years, had collapsed completely –

the proud city of Rome itself having been sacked twice by Vandals and other barbarians. The civilized were no match for the uncivilized once their military had been matched or exceeded in strength and numbers. The unspeakable, the unthinkable, became routine. Anyone who thinks that similar horrors cannot happen to us need only look at the Holocaust – an unthinkable crime on a vast scale, totally unanticipated by modern, civilized men and women.

Those obsessed with global warming should consider the consequences of even a small nuclear war. Nuclear war/ nuclear winter models developed by the National Academy of Sciences, the NASA Goddard Institute for Space Studies, and by various universities and think tanks (including Rutgers University's Department of Environmental Studies, the American Geophysical Union, the Journal of Geophysical Research, and Lawrence Livermore Laboratory), agree: a small nuclear war would punch a hole in the ozone layer that could be appallingly large, (depending on latitude) and would bring on a nuclear winter. Millions of tons of soot from burning cities would impact the ozone layer and block sunlight, causing a massive cooling that could reduce world temperatures to Ice Age levels. The degradation of farming and food supply, not to mention the collapse of world trade and of the world economy, could put tens of millions of humans in danger of starvation. World precipitation could be reduced by half – and millions could be killed or wounded from direct attack, completely overwhelming medical facilities and personnel in the victimized nations. Even if the worst of these expectations do not develop – because the number of weapons involved is smaller or the projections are askew

– enormous human suffering would result and radioactive particles would be wafted around the globe by prevailing winds. The earth and its atmosphere will have been poisoned to an alarming degree. The estimates by *Scientific American* were based on an assumed use of 100 nuclear bombs in a war between India and Pakistan. In the '90s, neither side had arsenals that large. To make the 100-bomb use more likely, the United States and China have both agreed recently to help India (U.S.) and Pakistan (China) get more uranium to build more bombs – in India's case by exempting that country from uranium purchasing restrictions on the world market, and in the case of Pakistan, by arranging its purchase of two additional nuclear reactors from China.

The prospects of a nuclear war, by design or accident, are multiplying rapidly because of failed leadership from the great nations of the world. All the great cities of the West – London, Paris, New York, Los Angeles, Rome – are at risk. The splendid historic buildings, irreplaceable art treasures, historic universities, teaching hospitals and research centers, business and banking headquarters, and the skills and expertise of millions of humans – physicians, artists, bankers, brokers, political and military leaders, religious and intellectual elites – could be obliterated in minutes. Civilizations could vanish. On point, Vladimir Putin recently remarked that Russia could destroy the United States in a half hour – and a few days later he received the first Confucius Peace Prize from Communist China!

What could the great democracies, with the aid and support of China, have done to prevent the situation we see developing today? They could have clamped down an economic blockade on Pakistan and India in the '90s to force them to stop development of nuclear weapons and admit UN inspectors to make sure the programs and facilities were permanently dismantled. Few, if any, nations in the world can tolerate a total economic blockade. Neither India nor Pakistan would have had any alternative than to cooperate with the UN and the world's strongest powers. This is also true today in regard to Iran and North Korea. Kim Jong Il in North Korea starved his people for decades while pouring his nation's resources into building a million-man army. That army has been the shield behind which he built his nuclear weapons. The UN estimates that tens of thousands of North Korean citizens have died from starvation and malnutrition, yet Kim got away with his policies. At almost any time, China could have intervened and stopped shipments of food and fuel to North Korea. Had China done that, the regime might have collapsed and all of Korea today might be a democracy and a safe, friendly trading partner for China. At the very least, North Korea would have had to stop its nuclear weapons program, dismantle what it had built, and let UN inspectors in on a regular basis to monitor compliance. This dark regime would have survived but there would be realistic expectations for gradual change and reform, even if it takes generations. Eventually, in some mutually approved way, the two Koreas might be reunited. But China has never used its leverage to significantly improve the situation, even when invited as a major participant in the six-party talks arranged by the Bush administration. As with Iran, a useful trading partner of China today, the Chinese have taken a Mandarin view of events, refusing to use their economic strength to prevent disaster while offering the excuse that an unstable North Korea might send millions of Korean refugees onto Chinese soil. This fallacious notion is undercut by the simple truth that the United States has within its borders a population of illegal immigrants that is likely equal to half the population of North Korea – and the U.S. is much smaller in overall population than China.

Russia has been even more short-sighted. Not only has Russia accelerated the dangers of war by helping rogue nations build nuclear facilities, it has also maintained a belligerent, bullying attitude toward the rest of Europe, brandishing its own oversized nuclear arsenal as a direct threat to Poland, Hungary, the Baltic states and other European nations. The KGB gang that runs Russia today, motivated by a still virulent Soviet era anti-Americanism, may very well be arming surrogates in the hope that they will bedevil Russia's great rival, thus finally winning the Cold War for Russia. Russia itself would not have to fire a shot. Russia is obviously the prime mover in the proliferation of nuclear weapons – and most of the beneficiaries are stridently anti-American (North Korea, Iran, Venezuela). Incredibly, Russia recently carried out military exercises which included a mock nuclear bombing of Warsaw. What could be more ominous?

NATO membership was extended to Poland, the Czech Republic and Hungary by the Clinton administration – which made sense in terms of Russia's threat to Germany. A buffer was established between "Soviet" lands and Germany, the powerhouse economy of Europe. Unfortunately, the Bush administration extended NATO into the Baltic countries (Latvia, Estonia, Lithuania) and there was open talk of bringing in Georgia and Ukraine and perhaps others bordering on Russia. This proved that neither Bush nor his advisors had ever read classic "balance of power" literature, like that written by Clausewitz: great powers should not have common borders.

Also unhelpful has been the behavior of Western European leaders. Both Chirac and Schroder were appeasers of Russia and of Saddam Hussein – and Schroder was later invited to sit on the board of one of Russia's giant energy industries (he also played the anti-American card to win his final re-election in Germany, a despicable act in light of all the sacrifices made by the United States to keep Germany safe and free over the half century following World War II).

Nevertheless, Russia's behavior since Vladimir Putin's rise to power has been irrational and dangerous. Russia's one real enemy, if it has one, is China, which shares a long border with Russia and which has ten times the population of Russia. The Chinese economy in recent years has overtaken those of Germany and Japan and is now second only to that of the United States. Chinese annual income is four times that of Russia and the differential is growing. Eventually that economic power will translate into military power and Russia will be facing a military and economic colossus all along the extended border of its sparsely settled Siberian and Asian territories, a treasure house of natural resources.

Russia's obvious course of action is to unite with the West and join Europe. As a member of the European Union it can outflank its old rival, the United States. If it ever joins NATO, it can seriously reduce America's influence within that military alliance. The Russian standard of living will rise if

Russia embraces Europe (a bear hug Europe may not entirely welcome but which it can't refuse) and Russia's economic fortunes will rise, given its huge resources of oil and natural gas. The abnormally expensive military posture aimed at Europe and America can be drawn down, with enormous savings to Russia – and membership in NATO would provide a shield against any future Chinese aggression. Why, then, doesn't Russia act rationally and help prevent the spread of nuclear weapons and the possibilities of nuclear war and nuclear winter? The answer, in a word, is Putin. A former president for eight years and prime minister for four, Putin has prevented President Dmitry Medvedev from seeking a second term in 2012 by taking the presidential prize for himself once again, but this time for two six-year terms (formerly the presidency was for four years, limited to two consecutive terms). It is widely understood that Putin was the power behind the throne during Medvedev's reign, despite Medvedev's often reasonable and friendly statements in his relations with the West. Medvedev and Putin have played good cop/bad cop with America and the West, but the truth is evident in the fact that Medvedev has stepped aside in 2012 to allow Putin, who is nearly sixty and eligible for the presidency until he is 71, to again take the helm. The mass of Russian people, trapped in a sham democracy, remain characteristically passive toward Putin's continuing dictatorship, although some people took to the streets in protest of rigged parliamentary elections in 2011.

During Putin's presidency there occurred secret police murders of journalists (including a woman journalist gunned down in her apartment lobby) and the assassination of expatriates (most sensationally, the radium poisoning of a renegade KGB agent, Alexander Litvinenko, then a British citizen). Putin will show his hand in future years as the godfather of the new Axis. Russia is also pushing for a new world reserve currency (to replace the American dollar), which it hopes to partner with China. This is part of a "new world order," which Russia hopes to co-found, according to Medvedev, with Communist China. Compare this vision of a world dominated by dictatorships to the 1945 Anglo-American "new world order" in Part II of this book. Despite China's long term threat to Russia and its Siberian energy resources, the Russians remain closer to China than to the West. Dictators stick together.

But what happens if nuclear weapons proliferate but are never used in anger? Will that mean the world will be at peace? Not likely, because nuclear weapons will make conventional warfare more likely.

The result of a full buildup of North Korean nuclear bombs and missiles is likely to be a second invasion of South Korea. Seoul, the capital of South Korea – with a metro population of over 20 million, almost half the population of that nation – is a glittering prize almost within reach of North Korean armies. Because of the placement of the cease fire line of 1953, Seoul is within artillery range of North Korea's swollen armies. A pincer attack on the city might bring it under Northern domination in days or weeks of hard fighting (fighting that would ruin much of the great city and kill tens of thousands). Prior to the North's development of nuclear weapons, such a course of action would have been unthinkable because the trip-wire presence of 28,000 American troops in South Korea meant that the American nuclear option would be available and likely to be used. North Korea would not have had a chance.

Now, due to the policies of three weak presidents, America's own cities, not to mention the 28,000 troops, would be at risk of incineration. Any threat to use our nuclear weapons would be checked by North Korea's obvious capacity to reply in kind. North Korea is crafting missiles that can hit American cities – all they need do is fit them with nuclear bombs. All of the immense advantages of American population, technology, industry and military force superiority have been squandered by our incompetent leaders.

The North Korean government is a totalitarian monarchy, dominated by military and police forces – a Stalinist throwback that has been an utter failure in almost every category except military power. Because it has nuclear weapons, even the likely successful defense of Seoul by South Korean forces could be met by the use of nuclear weapons to forestall defeat. Kim Jong Il was the son of the founding dictator of North Korea, Kim Il Sung, who engineered the invasion of South Korea in 1950, the beginning of a war that killed over two million people. The first Kim ruled until his death in 1994. He always yearned for a united Communist Korea, a legacy left to his son, Kim Jong Il, who passed it on to another relative within that secretive, militarized society, having set in motion a policy to make his youngest son, Kim Jong-Un, the next leader, thus preserving the monarchy. To do so he promoted the twenties-something son to a full general's rank in the armed forces. In the week the second Kim died, North Korea was begging for food aid again, promising again to stop enriching uranium – yet going ahead with ominous missile tests. The agreement to stop – for food or energy aid – has been a repeated tactic of North Korea, always dishonestly made. Whether the young and inexperienced Kim Jong-Un can survive the scrutiny of the pampered military in North Korea remains to be seen. At this point, anything may happen.

At the very least, North Korea's nuclear force, which should have been dismantled by China and the UN, will contribute to endless tensions and threats – rumors of war if not outright war. There will be crises that disturb the region and directly threaten America. It will be more than a headache, it will be a never-ending migraine – and that is the optimistic possibility. If China refuses to use economic pressures to push North Korea into nuclear disarmament, there is the very real possibility that, with or without U.S. help, South Korea, Japan, or both, may have to develop similar weapons. This would create a volatile situation, not unlike that of a nuclear-armed Israel facing a similarly armed Iran. That China cannot see this and act upon it – in its own self-interest if for no other reason – is beyond understanding.

Iran's endless threats to annihilate Israel foretell what that country may do with nuclear weapons. Israel's one large urban area away from Jerusalem is Tel Aviv, which has a metro population of three million, roughly half of Israel's population. Jerusalem is too sacred to Islam to be attacked with annihilating weapons, but Tel Aviv would be a prime target. One nuclear bomb would destroy most of the city and paralyze Israel. At present, Israel's elected prime minister is Benjamin Netanyahu, a hawk and seemingly the last person that would let such a thing happen, but Netanyahu is now being reined in by the Obama administration. Obama has apparently made up his mind to "contain" a nuclear armed Iran rather than to disarm it. Obama has shown little interest in pro-democracy, anti-dictatorship rallies in such countries as Iran, Syria and Belarus. He joined Britain and France in pouncing on the feeble Gaddafi in Libya, but shows little interest in bringing versions of democracy to Syria or Iran. Regarding Libya, one unfortunate truth, rarely noted by the media, is that Gaddafi gave up his programs for nuclear and other weapons of mass destruction after Anglo-American naval forces interdicted a shipment of bomb-making materials to Libya. These same countries mended relationships with Gaddafi but later turned on him and helped destroy him. Had he had the Bomb, they wouldn't have dared – a lesson not lost on Iran and North Korea today.

Even if Iran does not attack Israel (and Israel's ability to strike back might give it pause – keeping in mind, though, that Iran has ten times the population of Israel), the availability of nuclear weapons will inspire more belligerent behavior on the part of Iran toward the United States and toward Iran's near neighbors in the Gulf region. Iran already supports terrorists (Hezbollah, Hamas) near Israel and it maintains a strong hostility to Saudi Arabia and other Sunni Moslem countries (Iran is a Shia Moslem state and is Persian in language and ethnicity – not Arab). Saudi Arabia and Egypt, Arab Sunni states, may feel obligated to develop their own nuclear arsenals.

Once the nuclear weapons genii is out of the bottle, many other states with the scientific and industrial capacity to develop such weapons are likely to do so – both for self protection and for prestige. Turkey, Brazil, South Korea, Japan, perhaps even Nigeria or South Africa, will feel obligated to move in that direction. The NPT will have been effectively destroyed – due to the cowardice of China and the great democracies and the subversive, self-serving and hostile behavior of Putin's Russia.

The third crisis region will be Latin America, due to the growing belligerence and ambitions of Hugo Chavez and the arming of Venezuela by Russia.

A socialist movement is now stirring among predominantly Indian countries in South America, orchestrated by Chavez, who has made no secret of his Indio-centrist ethnic bias. Very poor states, including Bolivia and Paraguay, are joining Chavez in an extension of what Chavez calls "the Cuban Revolution," nationalizing industries, increasing state power, but also making serious efforts to bring minimal health and education standards to the poorest of the poor, a la Cuba. The problem, of course, is that socialism doesn't work as an economic system and democracy and authoritarian socialism are incompatible – the growing controls on media and the press in Venezuela proving the point. Worst of all, any state-based system will founder on Latin America's age-old problem: bureaucratic corruption. Philanthropy and Indian ethnocentrism have been the covers for Chavez' out of control ambitions. Like leftists everywhere, he excused his growing demands for control over the entire political, media and economic structure of his country by posturing as a Robin Hood figure. What Chavez' revolution was really about, as was Castro's, is personal egomania. Cuba today is a mere shadow of what it might have been under a more open, free, competitive and democratic system operating in cooperation with regional trading partners, including the United States, over a period of a half century. As in Venezuela today, the middle-class, backbone of prosperity in most democratic countries, was squeezed out by Castro who preferred the Soviet model – a political ruling class with wealth and privileges and a huge working class with shoddy goods, housing and food – and no intellectual or political freedom – subject to endless propaganda and ruthlessly cut off from any objective sources of information. In short, Cuba was and is a police state, and Venezuela, with or without Chavez, is headed in the same direction.

A leftist, heavily armed Venezuela will be a danger to its pro-American neighbor, Colombia. A nuclear-armed Venezuela will be a deadly danger to the United States. Again, economic boycott would stop the process and keep the region free of nuclear weapons. If Venezuela gets them, with Russian help, several other countries, including Argentina, Brazil and Chile may feel obliged to follow the same road. Atomic weapons could even be transferred to Cuba by Venezuela. The Cuban missile crisis of 1962, which brought the world to the brink of a massive nuclear war, should have been lesson enough to keep Latin America nuclear weapons-free. But it apparently hasn't, as three American presidents have done nothing effective about Hugo Chavez. Nature itself may make the difference as Chavez is now apparently a cancer victim, choosing Cuban surgeons rather than American ones to treat his ailment. Chavez' condition is unclear at this time and the political future of Venezuela without Chavez is impossible to track.

That these dictatorships will work together against the United States and other democracies is already a fact. Pakistan's nuclear scientists were helping North Korea on its bomb project and North Korea was shipping weapon-making materials to Burma and Libya. Pakistan also had nuclear ties to Libya and Iran. Chavez paid many visits to his counterparts in Russia, Cuba, Communist Vietnam and Iran. He was vocal in his support of North Korea. The new Axis is as global as the last one.

What is the most likely flashpoint for conflict instigated by or because of the new Axis? It is Korea. The other likely flashpoint is the Middle East, where an Israeli strike on Iran's nuclear weapons production facilities is possible if the United States and other great powers do not use economic power to halt Iran's weapons program. So far, the old diplomatic ploy of passing resolutions in the UN or even of instituting some feeble economic sanctions has been followed – accompanied by lots of hollow rhetoric from Barack Obama – but nothing has really been done to stop Iran from arming itself with nukes and the issue is coming to a head. By doing nothing in the economic blockade area, the powers may be dooming the Middle East to war. If attacked, Iran will unleash the thousands of rockets it has sent to Hezbollah fanatics in Lebanon, and Israel will be facing a war on its border, not to mention missile attacks and perhaps conventional air attacks from Iran. All of this bloodshed could be avoided if any of the three weak U.S. presidents had rallied the great democracies and, perhaps, China, to their logical peace-keeping duties.

Even if the nuclear weapons in the arsenals of the new Axis dictators are never used in anger, there is still the unacceptable possibility that such weapons, or some ingredients for the weapons, may be deliberately given to terrorists groups. Iran's sponsorship of Hezbollah strongly points in that direction. Nuclear weapons or radioactive terror bombs could do irreversible harm to the cities and economies of the democracies. Islamo-fascists have shown a murderousness not seen among ideological cranks since the Nazis. There is little doubt they would kill hundreds of thousands at one blow if they could. The Islamic terrorists who set off explosives in the basement of the Twin Towers in New York in 1992 admitted they were hoping the buildings would fall sideways, knocking down other skyscrapers and killing a quarter of a million people. In other words, they wished to inflict a nuclear bomb level of casualties on New York City. It is obvious that if they, or others like them, actually had such bombs, they would use them. The risk of terrorists getting radioactive bomb materials goes up exponentially when dictators who hate America are allowed to develop nuclear weapons. Another realistic danger is that nuclear weapons may be purchased or built by drug cartels, some of which are now in open warfare against the governments of Colombia, Mexico and Jamaica.

The week of the Pearl Harbor attack in December, 1941, *Life* magazine ran an article about the possibilities of war. The headline read, "U.S. Cheerfully Faces War with Japan." The article then pointed out that it would likely be a two-front war. You can't help but wonder if Americans would be so cheerful today if facing a nuclear Pearl Harbor on three or four fronts.

President George W. Bush's invasion of Iraq in 2003 was ostensibly to thwart Saddam Hussein's nuclear weapons program, but subsequent events showed that Saddam had no nuclear weapons program or any newly created weapons of mass destruction. There were signs that he was tooling up for something, but little had been accomplished.

A nuclear weapons program requires a huge infrastructure, as is evident now in Iran and North Korea. How is it that neither the CIA nor the world media had any inkling that the Iraqi infrastructure was missing? Because Bush assigned his military resources to Iraq, he couldn't deal with Iran, which obviously had a big nuclear weapons program going. Bush's hapless presidency, which involved not casting a veto for the first *six years* he was in office, will forever be remembered for the unnecessary Iraq war, which siphoned off precious resources while simultaneously exhausting public support for the use of force. Iraq, as some Democrat and Republican politicians and an American member of the UN inspecting team argued, could have been policed from the air. Saddam also could have been squeezed by tougher economic sanctions – though these were full of holes because Germany (Schroder) and France (Chirac) refused to comply – with some businessmen and some public officials from those countries taking bribes from Saddam, who was also raking in profits from the UN's food for fuel program, while starving his own people. The dictator certainly wanted to build nukes, but he didn't have the wherewithal in 2003. It was a delicate situation, but the center of Bush's attention should have been Iran, not Iraq.

Clinton, Bush and Obama have allowed this situation to develop. Hitler has the bomb because of them.

The world today is enjoying unprecedented economic development. India, China, Brazil, and various African countries are rising from poverty with expanded economic output, growth and wealth. If nuclear weapons can be kept out of the hands of dictators and the new Axis contained by wiser, more powerful nations, the outlook for the world is a good one. For that to happen, two nations, China and the United States, must step forward and make the difficult decisions necessary to prevent a Third World War. It can be done, but it will require courageous leadership. So far, that leadership has been lacking in both countries and both countries may pay a terrible price for their failure.

For three U.S. presidents to have allowed relatively small countries – countries so weak as to pose no real threat to the U.S. – to build the weapons with which they could destroy the U.S., is simply insane. Like the other three issues discussed here, this is a common sense issue. It is inconceivable that Ronald Reagan, John F. Kennedy, Dwight Eisenhower, Harry Truman or Franklin Roosevelt would ever have allowed this to happen.

So far, the worst president in American history has been James Buchanan, who did nothing to stop a slide into a horrible civil war that eventually killed more than 600,000 Americans. Casualties from a nuclear attack could easily exceed those of the Civil War.

It is impossible to think of any issue that defines the death wish more completely than this one. But Congress deserves its share of the blame. Where are the Republican Congressional voices on this surpassing issue? Where is the Republican leadership?

World Wars I and II were insane episodes of mass killing. There was no rational reason for either of these conflicts. A third world war would be worse than the other two together.

It must be prevented.

The total failure of the great powers, especially China, on this issue is baffling. China seems to want great power status when it comes to wealth and international respect, but not when it comes to leadership, risk-taking and sacrifice for a cause larger than China's own narrow self-interest. The entire planet and all of the people on it are vulnerable to the disasters of nuclear war, yet China, Japan, Germany and France (now joined by the new U.S. administration) are doing nothing as the doomsday clock ticks toward midnight.

This issue, the proliferation of nuclear weapons and the horrendous threat it proposes to human and animal life, to the planet and its atmosphere, to food supplies and world commerce, should be a major issue hammered at constantly by President Obama and other world leaders. Instead, we get Obama's weak and absurd references to "a world without nuclear weapons," while North Korea builds them. Just as FDR and Winston Churchill published and publicized the Atlantic Charter and the UN declaration, the leaders of the great democracies should publish a manifesto against the spread of nuclear weapons. They should fight for the non-proliferation treaty and help maintain it, using their vast economic resources to keep the treaty alive and working for the benefit of mankind. Some think an Israeli (or American) air strike would eliminate the Iranian nuclear threat. But others contend such a strike would delay the Iranian bomb only for a year or two. In truth, the issue is much larger than a bombing raid. It is *the* issue of our time and it should be a major focus of discussion by world leaders, world media, and the intelligentsia.

CONCLUSION: BARACK OBAMA AS THE EMBODIMENT OF THE GREAT LIBERAL DEATH WISH

The real significance of Barack Obama's election in 2008 is not that he was the first black American president, but that he was – in many of his attitudes - the first anti-American president. This is in contrast to what Colin Powell, a moderate Republican, would have brought to the political scene had he run and been elected the nation's first African-American president in 1996. Obama, it is clear now, was a stealth leftist in his presidential run. He pledged to be bipartisan, open and transparent, and he has been anything but. One would have to go back to Nixon to find a president as flagrantly dishonest and partisan as Obama. As a candidate, he obviously loved to talk, but didn't much care for dialogue or frank, honest exchanges of opinion. He kept his rhetoric general and bland throughout the 2008 campaign, carefully distancing himself from his religious mentor, the Rev. Jeremiah ("God damn America!") Wright and from his good friend, convicted terrorist Bill Ayers, who may have ghost-written Obama's memoir, *Dreams from My Father.*

Obama combines two traditions: the utopian leftism of academia with the tough machine politics of Chicago. This makes him the perfect embodiment of the Great Liberal Death Wish. His utopianism drives his idealism and his political machine background recommends the attitude that the end justifies the means. If Bill Clinton was ruined by Arkansas politics and might have done better by hanging out his law school shingle in Connecticut or some other relatively civilized place, Obama was ruined by Chicago and the strong identification he made with the notoriously corrupt political machine there. Michelle Malkin's best-selling book, *Culture of Corruption*, does a good job of examining that period in his life.

Obama's work as a community organizer in devastated Chicago south side neighborhoods, predominantly black and poor, also fueled his semi-socialist outlook. The dependency on government that he found there warped his sense of how government should operate. The population there is heavily dependent on government for food, housing, medical care and more. The mother and dad family (which Barack himself had scarcely experienced) has all but collapsed there.

There is also a psychological element in Obama's leftist orientation. Obama is half-white. Growing up he could have identified with the white side of the family, since he was largely raised by his white grandparents after age ten, or as a bi-racial person who could bridge the racial gap – or as a black. He chose the latter, as he explains in his autobiographical book, *Dreams from My Father*. Near the beginning of the book he explains that the task he undertook by writing it would be a search for his father, and, at the same time an effort to define his life as a *black* man. His African father, so important to Obama's sense of self, was a man he met once, on a brief summer visit.

Obama's childhood was peculiar and unsettling. His mother, oddly named Stanley after her father (who wanted a son) was a charming, intelligent and lively individual who seemed drawn to exotic foreigners, twice marrying foreign students, the first of whom was Obama's natural father. The senior Barack Obama was from Kenya and already married with two children, thus, according to American law, a bigamist when he married Ann (middle name) Dunham in Hawaii. Their son, born in 1961, was Barack, Jr.

Obama's mother was something of a maverick, announcing in high school that she would never marry or have children. Both of her marriages ended in divorce and Obama met his real father only that one time when the senior Obama visited Hawaii, which he had left years before. The marriage between Ann and Barack Sr. did not last a year and her second marriage to Lolo Soetoro, lasted but five years. She had a daughter, Maya, with Soetoro. Barack Obama lived in Indonesia for four years, then returned to Hawaii to live with his grandparents, Stanley and Madelyn Dunham. He was put into an exclusive prep school, which he attended from fifth grade to graduation at age 18. His mother went on to earn a PhD and became a respected anthropologist, but she went back to Indonesia when Barack was 16, staying there until he was 23, making only one summer visit home during that entire period. When she did return for good, in 1994, she was fatally ill with uterine and ovarian cancer and died about a year later, just short of her 53rd birthday.

As a result of this strange life, Barack hardly knew his real father, who became a mythical figure in his mind, lived with his foster father only four years, lost his mother for long periods in his life and was raised largely by his grandparents. This odd upbringing has been romanticized by many, including Barack himself in *Dreams*, but in fact, his mother's personality and actions doomed him to loneliness and introspection as to who he really was and where he really belonged. His emotional anguish is honestly expressed in *Dreams*, an engaging and well-written book (some say ghost-written by Ayers), but is provided by him with a flavor of internationalism, multiculturalism and other politically correct virtues that paper over the relationship failures, eccentric attitudes, and excessive independence that characterized his mother's behavior. He readily admitted, in interviews, to the sense of abandonment he felt as a boy. However Obama and others try to romanticize his early life, any objective observer would see that he had a dysfunctional childhood, bereft much of the time of both father and mother (and half-sister, Maya). He may have compensated, as many lonely children do, with the dreamy notion that he was special and had an important destiny.

Obama has said that his political orientation comes from his mother, who was the strongest influence on him in this regard (she supported FDR's New Deal and was, for the most part, a secular humanist). Ann Dunham's own dreams of raising a Third World citizen in her son left him with a conviction that he may be some kind of Third World person and prepared him for his self-identification with the impoverished blacks of Chicago's south side and the radical clergy and politicians who represented, worked, and lived with them.

Barack Obama did not live in the mainland U.S. until he was 18 years old. His alienation from the majority of

Americans may well have much to do with that, plus the fact that Hawaii is a multicultural, multiracial place with no ethnic majority. Living in Indonesia added to the lesson. Yet even in Hawaii and Indonesia, he was unusually sensitive about his race, as his autobiography indicates.

When Obama began digging into his real father's life and history he learned that his grandfather in Kenya had been arrested and sent to a prison camp during the Mau Mau uprising when the British still held Kenya as a colony. According to the grandfather's third wife (who left him) he was tortured by the British and their Kenyan allies despite being completely innocent. The source for this, Sarah Ogwel, Barack's step-grandmother, provided the information late in her life. This may explain why Obama had the bust of Winston Churchill removed from the White House and his view of Britain as tainted by the imperialism he felt had injured his father's father. His Indonesian stepfather's brother and father died in the fight for independence against the Dutch after World War II, and their family home was burned down. This may also have influenced Obama in an anti-European direction. When Obama visited Europe for the first time, he felt no attraction to it or identification with it, according to his autobiography.

Barack Obama Sr., who played so small a part in his son's life, was a committed socialist, but a lapsed Moslem. The younger Obama's stepfather, Lolo Soetoro, was also a lapsed Moslem. Nevertheless, Obama lived in a predominantly Moslem society for four impressionable years, age six to ten, and that may explain his impulse to reach out to the Moslem world today. He even went so far as to tell the new NASA director to make outreach to the Moslem world a priority for the space agency!

From his three parent figures, Obama received messages of socialism, a thin Moslem faith, a social rebelliousness (on the part of his mother) and a preference for the Third World and for minorities over the European world and the American majority. His remarks about the grandparents who raised him and paid for his private education are condescending and show little understanding of the virtues of their Midwestern heritage: hard work, discipline, Christian faith, self-sufficiency. Obama seemed to have little interest in traditional America, no pride in its remarkable historic achievements, and little appreciation of its unique place in world history. His prime concern growing up, as indicated in *Dreams*, was always himself.

What Obama is really good at is what his parents were good at: earning academic degrees. His African father graduated from college in Hawaii and earned a graduate degree at Harvard (before being dismissed from the school for unseemly private behavior). His mother went all the way to the doctoral degree at the University of Hawaii. Obama himself had an impeccable academic record, graduating from the well-regarded Punahou prep school and with honors from Columbia University, then finishing in the top ten per cent of his Harvard Law School class (also elected president of the Harvard Law Review, a signal honor).

In terms of the Peter Principle (the notion that in an organization each person rises to their level of competence but then is promoted to a higher level, one of incompetence) we can easily deduce that Bill Clinton could have moved from being governor of Arkansas to being a U.S. Senator from Arkansas without crossing the competence line; similarly, George Bush, as governor of Texas, had hit his mark and shouldn't have reached higher. In Barack Obama's case, since he showed a disinterest in permanently practicing law (he did so for four years), he might have become a professor in a prestigious law school like that of the University of Chicago, where he was a part-time lecturer for over a decade and was offered a position. He might also have become a college dean or even president of a prestigious small college, or simply stayed in the U.S. Senate to carve out a career as a left-liberal politician. President of the United States was a leap into incompetency for all three of them (as it was for Jimmy Carter).

Obama's credentials for the presidency are as thin as any in American history: three two-year terms in the Illinois state legislature and four years in the U.S. Senate – years he spent gearing up for his presidential run, voting "present" on many issues and missing scores of votes altogether. He developed the habit of voting "present" in the Illinois legislature, either to avoid taking a stand or because he didn't have a point of view. However, it has been pointed out that one president with a record almost as thin as Obama's was Abraham Lincoln, who served four terms in the Illinois legislature and only two years in the U.S. House of Representatives. Like Obama, he was also an attorney and a noted orator. But no one had any doubt about where Lincoln stood on the great issue of the day – the extension of slavery, whereas few could discern, when he was campaigning for the presidency, where Obama stood on anything. Lincoln also had military experience, having served in the Illinois militia. Most important of all, Lincoln had the common touch. His law practice was with small businessmen and average people. He got along well with working class and middle class folks, unlike Obama's two-tier orientation – to the academic elite and the marginalized poor. Obama does not know Middle America at all, as his 2008 campaign confrontation with "Joe the Plumber" indicated.

Obama worked for one year as an employee in the private business system – that's it. He had no other experience in the business world (his brief law career was not business-oriented), no administrative experience, no military service, no foreign policy experience, had never been a governor, and had almost no experience in Congress.

In terms of most of his elections (to the Illinois Senate, to the U.S. Senate, to the presidency) Obama has had a ridiculously easy time of it. George W. Bush paved the way for his successor so smoothly that almost anyone could have won the 2008 election for the Democratic Party. Obama ran as a mythic figure, a youthful Galahad who would save us from the recession, from global unpopularity, from wars abroad, and from educational and health systems that didn't serve all of us equally. He spoke in generalities, promising to be bipartisan and transparent, fair to all. Like Clinton, Nixon, and so many others who have run for president, he seemed to have inexhaustible energy for talking, traveling and campaigning. Obama won easily, with the full support of an admiring press and media corps, whose devotion to him and to his image has been aptly described by Bernard Goldberg in his book, *A Slobbering Love Affair: The True (and Pathetic) Story of the Torrid Romance Between Barack Obama and the*

Mainstream Media. He was and is the perfect example of the TV/primary candidate described in chapter one: elected because he looked and sounded good on television – and because people wanted a change. Had he been short, bald and an uncertain speaker, he would likely have lost to John McCain. Had people known how leftist he really is, he might have lost to McCain. It would be impossible for anyone as unprepared by experience as Obama to win the highest office in Britain, Canada, Australia or any democratic European country. Only America is foolish enough to elevate amateur TV performers to the presidency.

With almost no qualifications for the job, how has Obama done ?

Sensibly, as a minority president from the far left spectrum of the Democratic Party, it would have behooved him to spend his first two years building widespread support by reaching out to Republicans, the elderly, and the white majority. He could have done this by inviting the chastised Republicans (down 255-178 in the House and 60-40 in the Senate) to cooperate on some popular health care reforms, such as plugging the "doughnut hole" in Medicare prescription coverage (which is a disaster for about a quarter of the elderly population) and adding some of the regulatory changes that emerged in the swollen Obamacare bill, namely those relating to pre-existing conditions and continuation of coverage. These would have been very popular and would have enlisted at least some Republican congressional support.

Announcing that the Mexican border had to be closed before any "comprehensive" solution could be found to the immigration crisis would have laid the groundwork for

Republican concessions later on some kind of amnesty. Instead, Obama adopted the disastrous policy of suing Arizona for doing what the federal government is obliged but has refused to do. This alienated the majority there and inspired other states to adopt bills similar to Arizona's. Also, Obama could have been careful to choose a centrist for his first nomination to the Supreme Court, someone most Republicans could support with approval, if not enthusiasm. Judge Sonia Sotomayer, his first pick, has now become a leftist activist on the court, in effect a Democrat politician placed there to pass liberal legislation. His second nomination, that of Elena Kagan, was not much better.

To build popularity with those who did not vote for him and to enlist Republican cooperation on a range of issues, Obama would have to have chosen a chief of staff known to be bipartisan. Instead, he chose Rahm Emanuel, an old crony from the Chicago area political machine known for his keen partisanship and relentless drive to win on his terms. That was the first misstep. Instead of looking at his presidency as an eight-year, two-term one that would have to be launched with good will toward the opposition, he and Emanuel seem to have concluded that they would take advantage of their majorities in both houses of Congress to ram through as much radical legislation as they could in the first two years before losing their wide margin of superiority in the mid-term elections. In doing so, they alienated and alarmed the voting majority and lost the support of independents.

Going for a two-year presidency rather than an eight-year one was a serious mistake. The first two years of his *second* term should have been the target period for big ticket liberal items. Instead, he faces the possibility of being another failed one-term president, like Jimmy Carter. Getting reelected now trumps radicalism for Obama – a fact likely to alienate his left wing even more than his failures have. The Wall Street "occupiers" are an indication, in part, that the far left is unhappy with Obama. Even if reelected in 2012, Obama is not likely to have a Democrat House of Representatives or a veto-proof majority in the Senate, hence his second term will inevitably be one of antagonistic gridlock.

Partisanship, in direct violation of his campaign pledges, characterized Obama's first two years. He quickly became one of the most divisive presidents in modern history. Instead of seeing politics as a two-way street, in which bipartisanship and compromise are necessary, Obama seemed to read his election as a plebiscite which endowed him with near-dictatorial powers. After Nancy Pelosi and her House colleagues had come up with a 2000+ page health care bill, Obama loftily announced he wanted it signed and on his desk in three weeks, less time than would be required for anyone to read it. Whether his arrogance is a defense mechanism or an adjunct to his conviction that he has a special and important destiny, it is one of his most irritating traits.

In one 2008 campaign speech, adopting a folksy vocabulary fit for his audience, discussing doctors he said that if you went to one with a minor foot ailment, that doctor might say to himself, "Well, if I cut this foot off" (or words to that effect), "I'll make a lot more money!" It was amazing to hear a presidential candidate say anything so silly.

Another important trait is dishonesty. To put it another way, Obama, like many politicians, is a skilled public liar. We have him on TV tape telling smaller audiences a few years ago that he favors the Canadian "single payer" (government health insurance) system and he hopes government insurance will replace private health insurance in the United States over a period of ten to twenty years. Yet, when confronted later, he denied that he favors the Canadian system. He also lied about whether Americans could keep their present health insurance and doctors under Obamacare, shouting in endless speeches, "You can keep your health insurance and your doctor!" Yet he knew full well that the Obamacare bill has built-in incentives to encourage employers to drop their health insurance coverage of employees and pay the fine for doing so, as the fine is less costly than the health insurance. Obamacare is a major step toward socialized health insurance, a la Canada – and Obama knows it and lies about it.

Obama also lied about costs for health care not going up. As with Medicare, costs will skyrocket as they always do when the government is paying the bills. This will lead directly to rationing of service, as in Canada and Britain, and long delays in scheduling surgeries and in getting into hospitals (Britons wait weeks or months to do so). People can die under this approach, as they sometimes do in Britain , especially if they are elderly. This is the opposite of the free enterprise health care system in America, where even the elderly who are very ill have quick access to surgeries and hospital care, paid for by their private health insurance plans or by government plans piggy-backed onto the private sector, as Medicare is. Failure to do so is the exception, rather than the rule, in the U.S., given America's multiple private insurance plans.

Obama got his medical care bill passed through parliamentary trickery ("reconciliation," which was dubbed "the nuclear option" when Republicans contemplating using the maneuver), with the House not passing its version at all, but accepting the Senate bill with none of the usual bargaining between the two houses. At various stages the winning votes came late at night, on Christmas Eve, etc., and with no Republicans in House or Senate on board – unique in the history of major social reform bills. By the time the bill was finally passed, many months after Obama had arrogantly demanded it, a solid majority of Americans opposed the bill – and a majority favors its repeal today.

Obama and members of his administration are now in danger of encouraging racial animosities – an effort inherent in the federal law suit against Arizona for making a mild effort to identify illegal aliens among those stopped by police for law violations. Obama seems to have little appreciation of the give and take necessary in a two-party democracy. He is thin-skinned and has hinted many times that if he thought he could, he would curtail free political speech on Talk Radio. His instincts are for more power and he seeks the kind of top-heavy government and excessive taxation and regulation that have slowed the economies of Europe to a crawl. Ominously, in a recent survey a significant majority in the U.S. now describe Obama as a socialist.

Obama came of age in the '70s, when anti-establishment attitudes were at their peak, celebrated in pop music and movies (the age of "Mash"). These were Lyndon Johnson's Great Society years – massive federal programs to eliminate poverty, grandiose plans (at grandiose expense) to remake society. Obama's agenda runs back to that period and it is a tired, old-fashioned, out of date one: a longer school year because we are supposedly falling behind other countries; subsidies for high speed trains, so we can be more like Europe; socialized health insurance (Canada) or, even worse, socialized medicine (Britain); Government-subsidized college education for all; more and more government controls on the economy; higher taxes; anti-military attitudes reflecting the Vietnam debacle; and anti-Republican attitudes reflecting Watergate. All of this was compounded in the '70s and after by anti-business attitudes resulting from the rise of what some call the New Class: academics (mostly government-employed) and government bureaucrats. On top of this a strong secularization was proceeding both from the courts and from an enthusiastically libertine Hollywood that often pilloried businessmen.

Obama seems to hold all these attitudes dear, despite that he is over 50 now, not the teenager he was in the late '70s. With each new policy recommendation, reflecting the stale agenda of the left in the '70s, he exhibits a spectacular lack of common sense. His projected and current levels of debt could drive America into bankruptcy and federal controls on credit are likely to stifle investment and growth. He clearly wants taxes to increase substantially, a recipe for continuing recession.

With Obamacare, he seems either indifferent to or ignorant of the fact that his plan will bring about a historic shift away from the doctor/client model, based on a consumer/provider relationship, to a government endowment of medical care, which puts the patient in the psychological and very likely the actual situation of being a welfare recipient waiting in line for service, clutching his ticket number. He also seems not to anticipate (or to admit) that rationing of service will not only be inevitable, but necessary. With any single payer system (which always means a government system, since no single health insurance company can pay everyone's bills) the payer runs out of money. This is because the payer has to pay all kinds of other bills (defense, highways, national parks, postal service, retirement benefits, and all the other government programs run by government agencies). In Vancouver, thousands of surgeries, including heart surgeries, had to be postponed because of the costs incurred by the British Columbia government in hosting the Winter Olympics.

That Obama may, indeed, be well aware that rationing is inevitable and that he is covering up the fact, was his sneaky appointment (during the brief Fourth of July recess in 2010) of Dr. Donald Berwick as the new director of Medicare and Medicaid. Berwick, who resigned under pressure in late 2011, publicly declared his love for the unattractive British health care system and openly embraced the notion of rationing of care. Obama knew that Berwick's hearings before a Senate committee would be contentious, so he snuck him in by abusing the recess appointment mode (to be used only when Congress is in recess for long periods, as it used to be, but not simply over a brief vacation). Berwick saw medical care as a top-down gift from the government, an authoritarian endowment, with no room for market forces. His appointment was a strong signal of what is to come and Americans will be livid, perhaps desperately so, when they personally experience what is to come in health care.

As the free enterprise medical care system (which over 80% of Americans approved of in a recent survey) is dismantled, fewer of the best and brightest will go into medicine. The hard-driving, entrepreneurial male doctors we have known and admired for so many decades, will begin to phase out, as incomes are squeezed and government paperwork, restrictions, and red tape increase. More and more doctors will be foreigners, as in Britain, and more of them will be nurse practitioners, because there will be a shortage of physicians.

The people who need medical assistance the most, the elderly, will suffer the cruelest cuts. Obamacare cuts a half trillion dollars from Medicare providers, hurting Medicare Advantage plans, in order to pay for the huge increases in Medicaid and other programs. It is, essentially, a shift of resources away from the elderly (who are mostly white) to the young and indigent (who are more likely to be black or Hispanic). In combination with a philanthropic immigration system that may amnesty millions of Hispanics, it will tie the federal government (and the states) down with massive new outlays. In fact, neither the federal government nor the state governments will be able to bear the burden of Obamacare, which is why it will have to be deconstructed by future presidents and Congresses.

Obama seems convinced that most Americans will love Obamacare once they see how it operates. He acknowledges that many Americans have been upset at "the process" that established it, but brushes this off, not realizing that "process" is exactly at the heart of what is wrong with his politics: for him, the end justifies the means. It is all right to lie to get something, to dissemble, misrepresent and hide details, as long as the goal is high-minded.

None of this had to happen. Paul Ryan, the bright young Republican Congressman from Wisconsin, has put forward many interesting ideas to improve medical care, though his bid to end Medicare for those under 55 was a major political blunder, undermining 2012 support from seniors who had voted heavily Republican in 2010.

The renowned Cleveland Clinic, one of the very best heart and cancer hospitals in the nation, has pioneered administrative and medical delivery systems – reforms that could be adopted more widely. Medical Savings Accounts, as Ryan has explained in his Patient's Choice Act (see his web site), would give patients some freedom in how their medical money is spent and would help keep some elements of the market in play. Allowing health insurance companies to cross state lines, to continue plans for those who have left employment (portability), to stress preventative care, to artfully mix free enterprise with government-sponsored programs, to extend the time limits for private coverage under COBRA (perhaps for up to five years of coverage), to give doctors and patients more freedom and more options, and many other reforms are possibilities not considered under Obamacare, which is stifling, heavy-handed, and will, in the long run be unacceptably costly. Medicare is already bureaucratic, blindly imposing rules and having little or no flexibility in making exceptions for those who have made honest mistakes in meeting deadlines and the narrow windows for participation.

America now spends about 15% of its gross income on medical care. Liberals and socialists grouse about this as though we were spending 15% of national income on recreational drugs or Las Vegas vacations. America has been cutting edge in medical technology (and new technology is the main reason for increasing costs, a rarely understood aspect of the situation), and if we choose to make these new technologies available to all, what of it? Americans spend billions annually on swimming pools, bowling, marijuana, pornography. If we choose to spend 15% or even 20% on medical care, that is our business and there is nothing immoral about it – quite the opposite. Our ill, including the elderly, can have the world's best care quickly and efficiently, with no long waits for government approval.

We do have a problem with a relative few, perhaps one to three per cent of the population according to studies, who cannot purchase affordable health insurance: They are not poor enough for Medicaid, old enough for Medicare, or they are self-employed or employed by companies too small to make insurance available to employees. Obviously something has to be done for these people. Governor Romney managed to get a universal health care bill passed in Massachusetts, working with a Democrat legislature, and it fills these gaps, though it has been troubled by inflation in costs. Answers for this problem will not be easy, but the absolutely essential thing is to retain our free enterprise health care system and our mostly free enterprise health insurance system – regulated in the public interest by Congress. The systems in Canada and (especially) in Britain, would be unacceptable in America.

Congress could and should separate Medicare and Social Security budgets from the general budget, with no Social Security or Medicare payroll taxes ever used for other purposes. Most Social Security and Medicare costs, each year, are paid from their own payment systems, with only the shortfall picked up by the federal government – and only these shortfalls should be listed as federal expenses, keeping in mind that Congress "borrowed" trillions from the Social Security fund over the decades when Social Security accounts were running surpluses. A modest Medicare-only federal sales tax, in addition to ongoing payroll tax support, might also be a way to fund future Medicare costs.

Obama's eagerness to spend trillions of dollars the government doesn't have is reflected in the silly recommendations he has made in non-health areas. Parts of the bloated "stimulus" package, which ran to nearly $800 billion, were various longtime Democrat pork projects, including $8 billion for new high speed rail systems. This is seed money only, as a true high speed rail system would cost hundreds of billions. Worse, such a system would require huge annual federal and state subsidies to stay afloat. This is money neither the federal nor state governments have or will have. Europe has marvelous fast trains, as we all know, but Europe is also much smaller than the U.S. in area and much denser in urban development. Obama hyped the new trains in Spain, as well as other "infrastructure" projects there, but many of these, including an enormous airport, have become white elephants, abandoned because they meet little or no need or because they were prohibitively expensive. Citing Spain is an example of Obama's naivete and his lack of understanding of economics.

Commercial passenger rail services disappeared here because they were not cost effective. Our feeble Amtrak system requires large subsidies, which most Americans seem content to pay, but an all-new system on a much larger grid, would be prohibitively expensive. Only a very few American passenger train routes make money, Washington to New York and Boston to New York, among them.

Within urban areas, rail transit works best when it goes from one essentially pedestrian-oriented environment (like an airport) to another (like a downtown, with its hotel, convention, and shopping facilities). Americans are not keen on train trips that are more expensive than driving. The disadvantages inherent in rail systems, as modern and "New Urbanist" as they may appear, have been pointed out in numerous studies, including those of Wendell Cox on his Demographia website. "New Urbanist" city planning also has the serious flaw of significantly driving up housing costs, as Cox and his staff have shown in repeated studies. These notions of Obama regarding land use and transportation go straight back to the Great Society and its failed policies. They indicate again how little understanding Obama has of the essential American temperament or of economic realities in the 21st century.

Tax-payer funded college education for everyone, or almost everyone, is another boondoggle idea advanced by Obama. Like Obamacare, it would shift an enormous annual expense from private payment to public (taxpayer) payment. It would also double or triple the present costs by adding nearly the entire high school population to the college rolls.

The traditional four-year college education is now completed by about a quarter of Americans – which is about right. Anyone who teaches at the college level knows that even many of these students don't really belong in college. To accommodate nearly everyone, the college level of instruction would have to be degraded to the high school level. Certain professions: law and medicine, teaching and scientific pursuits, engineering and architecture, geology and chemistry, require a college education. Also, despite the enormous expense, some people enjoy a four-year liberal arts education as a kind of finishing school, to polish their literary or historical interests, to refine the mind and enlarge intellectual horizons. But the cost of higher education today, even at public colleges and universities, makes this a luxury most cannot afford (and that most would not be interested in, anyway).

Community colleges make a lot more sense as a track for continuing education. America's two-year colleges are among the best in the world and are famous for being student-oriented. Currently they are booming because they tie higher education to vocational education. A graduate from a community college with an AA degree not only has taken some general courses, in English, social studies and science, but has a major in a vocational field: which can be anything from accounting to air-conditioning mechanics, dental hygiene to computer tech, hospital management to law enforcement. Teachers in the community colleges are, by and large, not forced into the publish-or-perish mode that university professors suffer with and are expected to put their time and energy into classroom teaching, rather than research. Lopping off the senior year of high school to get some students into community colleges a year earlier is worth considering.

At present, American students and their parents pay about two thirds of college expenses and use student loans for the remaining third. Given this reality, there is absolutely no reason why American taxpayers should be billed for everyone's college tuition. It is an awful idea and one that would swell college ranks with those who don't belong there and are better off employed full-time. One of the characteristics of the New Class, of which Barack Obama is an exemplar, is the notion that everyone is like they are. Whatever credentials they have in life are college-earned: academic achievement and academic styles of leadership are all they know. Therefore, everyone should have a college degree (and, undoubtedly, eventually a graduate degree). The thinking seems to be that if everyone goes to kindergarten, everyone should go to college.

Obama and those like him don't seem to understand that society needs really capable auto and airplane mechanics; that we need skilled construction workers, electricians, plumbers, sales people, clerks, police officers, pilots, soldiers, accountants, maintenance men, postal workers, delivery people, factory workers, restaurant employees, managers of all kinds, and a vast host of other workers who have no particular need for a college education. There are countless successful entrepreneurs (Rush Limbaugh being a prime example) who did not go to college. People who start small businesses (the primary source for new jobs in America) may need a little professional training, but not much. The main thing for them is to know their business and to know the public. The men and women who repair furnaces, air conditioning systems, automobiles, and other machines we use in daily life are crucial to the smooth functioning of our society – and generally they are well paid and have a strong work ethic. College education for all is a foolish idea and one the nation cannot afford and does not need.

Education is an obsession with liberals, who are sure it will solve all problems and help bring about utopia. What it brings about, among other things, is the New Class (what author David Lebedoff calls "the New Elite"), a horde of know-it-all types disconnected from the business world and the real world in general, but sure they have been anointed to run everything. Obama loves to appoint these types to every commission and department with openings. They are the multiculturalists, the enforcers of speech codes and political correctness, and the libertine/libertarian folks who live in enclaves of their own. They are also the "czars" he appoints to avoid Congressional oversight on administrative appointments.

Such people are forever shouting that American education is a disaster. Back in the 1950s, when the Russians got into space first, with Sputnik, a loud cry arose that Soviet Russia was graduating enormous numbers of "scientists and engineers," and we were not. We were falling hopelessly behind. It took decades before *Time* magazine eventually admitted that all those scientists and engineers were mostly lower level technicians, but by that time we had passed the "National Defense" highway-building act and the "National Defense" student loan program (the idea being that it would help us catch up with the Russians in education). What had happened, apparently, is that the Russians had done better with their captured German scientists than we did with ours, but once our attention was focused we caught up quickly and put men on the moon in 1969 and several times after, an engineering and technical feat still unmatched by any other nation, including Russia.

The annual American economic output is in the neighborhood of $16 trillion, even in a recession – far ahead of second place China and third place Japan and far, far ahead of any of the rest of the world's 200 nations. America has dominated Nobel Prizes for decades and leads the world in many technical fields including in medical and military innovations, not to mention the invention and expansion in use of the personal computer and the Internet. Given these realities, our schools can't be all bad.

The notion that we need more hours to the school day or more days to the school year, endorsed by Obama, goes back a few decades to comparisons that were made with the Japanese school year. What no one understood at the time (including those big corporations that bought message ads in U.S. newsmagazines) is that the Japanese were counting Saturdays in their total number of school *days*, because Japanese workers worked half-days on Saturday, as Americans once did, and Japanese students went to school half days on Saturdays. The enthusiasts for more school days also didn't understand or know that the Saturday half-days were being phased out, one at a time, so that Japanese workers and students would have an American style "weekend." The number of Japanese school days was inflated by these misunderstandings. The alarmists touting European schools, did not know that the European school day ends about 1 p.m. in many countries, and that many students move into work-study apprenticeship programs around age 16, often attending school only one day a week, while putting in four days on the job.

The bottom line on all this is that Americans spent (and still spend) more hours in school than most people around the world, while more Americans go to college, proportionately, than do people in any other country. President Obama's take on this old fraud is to hold up South Korea as an example we should emulate. South Korea does have a lot of school days, but Americans spend more time in class than South Koreans – in fact, have more hours of instruction than any students in the world. Europe, North America and Japan seem to get along fine with the present number of school days and, since America's school day is longer, we have little to worry about. In addition, much in the Japanese system is based on rote memory – the Japanese having copied the old Prussian educational system over a century ago. In any event, schools cannot magically transform undisciplined and unmotivated students into college scholarship winners. Students and their parents are as important to success in school as teachers, and perhaps more so. This is lost on the social engineers who believe that pouring money into school systems will make all the difference. The best student achievement scores regularly come from states like Utah, North and South Dakota, Nebraska, and Iowa, where costs are kept down and teachers' salaries are often modest.

As for summer vacation, it is more necessary now than ever. The one area in which Europeans really are ahead of us is in granting vacation days to working adults. Four weeks is normal in Europe – and Finland has six weeks of guaranteed, annual paid vacation, as against two in the U.S., a day or so less than even the Japanese. American working parents should have more summer vacation to share with their children. The host of summer camps, summer jobs and other activities (including summer school for some students) that American young people traditionally enjoy, fills up the summer months and provides most of them (and most of their exhausted teachers) a real break from school and a fresh start in the fall. Social engineers like Obama may not like it, but most Americans do. It should be noted that when a system-wide year-round school program was tried in Los Angeles, it was a flop, universally rejected by students, parents and teachers.

Obama's wild spending, combined with vast new entitlements, means that he will eventually have to make large federal budget cuts to avoid falling into bankruptcy, hyper-inflation, or both. It seems obvious that for him, these cuts will come from the military, including research and development. He doesn't seem to have much enthusiasm for democracy itself, as his tepid support of the anti-government protestors in Iran strongly suggests. We cannot export our way of life or impose it on others, he has said. Vigorous, embattled little democracies like South Korea and Taiwan, not to mention Israel, seem hung out to dry by this administration. This may be because Obama seems more interested in socialism than in democracy. Socialism is identified with *equality*, democracy with *freedom* – and in a free society, some do better than others.

Obama seems to have no faith in the group he has identified with: African-Americans. He seems convinced they can never compete with the immigrant groups or with white Americans. Because they can't make it on their own, government, acting in the philanthropy/permissiveness mode, will provide everything – housing, medical care, better education, food stamps. For Obama, taxes must go up to pay for all his entitlement programs.

Higher taxes, cuts in Medicare and the military, a vast expansion of entitlements, growing government bureaucracies and government regulations, will flatten economic growth so that the U.S. will end up more like Europe: low growth, high unemployment, overgrown bureaucracies. It could be worse: we could go bankrupt, unable to pay the interest on the enormous debts being run up (debts covered by our Chinese, British and Japanese lenders). The highest federal deficit in history was the last year of the Bush administration: a half trillion dollars. Obama averaged three times that – one and a half trillion – for each of his first two years. He cheerfully projects trillion dollar annual deficits for years to come – and that doesn't count the enormous Obamacare expenses that will be coming along soon – and deliberately underestimated by those who passed it.

On many issues, Obama, in his misplaced self-righteousness, has pushed policies the general public disagrees with: from granting civil trials to non-citizen terrorists to suing Arizona for trying to stop the invasion across its borders. Will Obama be as politically intelligent as Bill Clinton, and warm to the majority he now ignores? It doesn't appear so. Obama provided no leadership on the budget impasse, preferring his "leading from behind" mode – which is to say, not leading at all, but expecting others to do the work. Clinton was a centrist to begin with, while Obama is left-wing by choice. Very likely, with reelection paramount in his thinking, Obama pursued an anti-Republican Congress campaign line (forgetting that he had both houses of Congress for half his term and the U.S. Senate for all of it), looking forward to reelection in the Harry Truman 1948 mode and the restoration of a Democrat-controlled Congress in his second term. The ruthlessness with which he acted on health care and other policies while he had a solid Democrat majority tells us all we need to know about how he would govern in a second term with a Democrat Congress. The 2010 election has been a sharp rebuke of Obama's domestic policies and methods, but does not rule out his re-election in 2012, so adept is he at projecting a media image.

If anything, Obama is even worse in foreign policy than in domestic policy. Woodrow Wilson had a dream of a world dominated by democracies working together to prevent war through collective security. The dream was premature, but it was noble – and it inspired every president after him, especially Franklin Roosevelt and Ronald Reagan. Obama has the worst of Wilson's qualities: stubbornness, self-righteousness, runaway idealism – but he lacks Wilson's vision for a world of democracies in which the only warfare is economic competition within a system of free trade.

Obama's foreign policy so far has been based on the premise that America is disliked in the world and to amend that we must become apologetic and weaker. As mentioned earlier, he went through a silly exercise of "re-setting" America's policy with Russia, not realizing that any problems we had with Russia and its clients were based on Russian perfidy, not a lack of good will on the part of the United States. Obama seems oblivious to the dangers posed by the new Axis and has relied on meaningless sanctions and diplomatic folderol to counter its growing strength.

The notion held by liberals and leftists that America must be loved by the rest of the world betrays their short memory. In the 1950s and '60s, after participating in the world's greatest war against tyranny, then checking the ambitions of Stalin while wholeheartedly backing the anti-colonial freedom movement in the Third World, the U.S. was rewarded with "Yankee go home" signs on different continents, plus anti-American riots. Few (especially liberals) remember how popular Soviet Russia's two bumpkin co-dictators, Nikita Khrushchev and Nikolai Bulganin, were – when the stubby pair were known as "B&K" – and hit the road on visits to various parts of the world. No "Russki go home" signs were in evidence, despite the repressive Soviet Empire in Eastern Europe. President Kennedy went to the brink of war over Cuba, greatly expanded American armed forces (even calling up the reserves over Berlin) and upped the military ante in Vietnam - yet turned the popularity issue in our favor. Whether other countries love us or not is relatively unimportant as far as the self-interest and survival of the democratic countries is concerned. It was not a big issue with Ronald Reagan (or Theodore Roosevelt, for that matter).

In all likelihood, Vladimir Putin and the other authoritarians see Obama as a weakling, and will act accordingly.

On the four issues raised in this study, Obama is a failure on all four. He would not change the party nominating system because he used it to get elected; he will do nothing meaningful about immigration because he is getting the votes

– the borders will remain open while Obama seeks citizenship amnesty for illegals; far from reducing judicial activism by federal judges, he encourages it – and his appointments to the Supreme Court have been liberal activists; finally, as noted, he is doing little or nothing to stop the new axis of dictators from building nuclear weapons and making them available to fellow dictators.

Is there any doubt, then, that Obama fulfills the best definition of "the great liberal death wish"? The possibilities of his abandoning the dogmas of the New Class – of which he is a dedicated member – are slight.

Of the four major candidates for president in the U.S. in 2008, the least fit for the job was Obama. Mrs. Clinton would have made a better president; John McCain would probably have been a better president than Secretary Clinton; Governor Romney, with his broad background in business and administrative government, would be a better president than McCain. Consequently, the best candidate of the four wasn't even nominated, while the least of the four was elected president. This proves that something is very wrong with our system for selecting presidential nominees. In his first term, Obama had three major policy directives: a stimulus package of some $800 billion that did little good (economic growth in 2011 was an anemic 1.7%); he continued the bailout of financial institutions begun by President Bush (which did seem to help); and he snuck Obamacare through Congress despite majority disapproval. After that, he spent most of his time campaigning, vacationing, and playing golf. Rarely has a president had such an empty record – and we will see more of the same in any second term.

Unless the American economy can achieve growth rates of at least 3 or 4%, the shortfalls in government income will continue to be a quarter to a third of the federal budget, creating levels of debt that will lead to interest obligations that will be impossible to maintain. An essentially anti-business ideologue like Barack Obama will have no answers to the inevitable defaults that will follow.

PART II

WHAT IS AT STAKE: ANGLO-AMERICAN CIVILIZATION

ANGLO-AMERICAN REVOLUTIONS

During 1688-89 England experienced a political revolution that changed the world. A Catholic monarch, James II, was overthrown by his Protestant opponents within and outside England. A Dutch fleet brought the king's daughter, Mary, and her husband, William of Orange (also the king's nephew), from the Netherlands to London and the throne. Dubbed "the Glorious Revolution," in part because there was little or no bloodshed, the change of monarchs was accompanied by political and philosophical changes in the nature of English government – changes that influenced other revolutions, including the American one about a century later. The Catholic king had outraged parliament, the universities, the courts, and the English church and its bishops, by his high-handed behavior. His outlook was increasingly one of a continental tyrant, rather than a monarch respectful of Parliament and other institutions in England.

James II quit almost without a fight, it is true, but with French help he did make a stand later in Ireland, so the revolution was not exactly bloodless. Losing the struggle in Ireland he fled to France for the rest of his days. The English are also fond of saying that their island resisted foreign invasion from 1066 to the present, but Dutch troops made up a large part of the force accompanying William and Mary (who became co-monarchs), and Dutch warships carried the expedition across the channel.

Safe for Protestantism and Queen Elizabeth's state church, England began to institute changes demanded by the Protestant factions in Parliament. The events and legislation of 1688-89 are known collectively as the Glorious Revolution and include a Bill of Rights and limits on the monarchy, thus preventing the kind of "absolute" monarchy then existing in Russia, France and other continental nations. The English Bill of Rights had a powerful influence on the American Bill of Rights 100 years later. The English bill established a kind of contract between king and people, in which certain "natural rights" were either reaffirmed or put in statute terms for the first time. Parliament first passed a Declaration of Rights, then refined it into a Bill of Rights. The philosophy of rights strongly reflected the views of "social contract" political philosophers, especially those of John Locke, as expressed in his famous work, *Two Treatises of Civil Government.*

The social contract idea had been posed earlier by an English pessimist, Thomas Hobbes, and later, by a French optimist, Jean Jacques Rousseau. It forms the basis for the notion of sovereignty in the American Constitution of 1789 ("We, the people ...). Hobbes conjectured that primitive men had come together for protection and survival, designating a leader who had responsibilities to the group or tribe, and to whom members of the group had reciprocal duties. Locke was more optimistic and argued that men had come together, not under duress, but freely, to form a government and choose a sovereign. The revolutionary note in Locke's thinking was that if the sovereign did not meet his responsibilities, the group could divest him of his power. Later, Rousseau and Jefferson were in agreement on this point – and it forms the main line of argument in Jefferson's *Declaration of Independence*.

The English Bill of Rights, emerging from the Glorious Revolution, reaffirmed certain English rights that could be traced all the way back to Magna Carta in 1215, and which were later written into various law codes, common law decisions, court rulings, and the like – reflecting the fact that the English had a long struggle with autocratic kings who violated these rights and who were determined not to be bound or limited by them.

The events of 1688-89 and the English Bill of Rights added or reaffirmed such basic rights as freedom of political speech, freedom from excessive bail and cruel punishments, trial by a jury of peers, a right to bear arms and to be free of a standing army and its threats to liberty, the rights of Parliament (to be elected regularly and to have the power of the purse), curtailments of the king's power in regard to taxation and to calling or dismissing Parliament, freedom of petition, religious freedom for Protestants (including non-Anglicans, who made up a sizable chunk of the English population at that time, though not for Catholics and Jews), and no regal interference in the making of laws and the authority of the courts.

The long list of grievances under King George III cited by Thomas Jefferson in the *Declaration of Independence* is closely modeled on the similar list of grievances against King James II at the time of the English Bill of Rights, and in some cases the same phrasing is used by Jefferson.

Madison's American Bill of Rights echoes the English Bill in several particulars, including the quartering of troops, trial by jury, the right to bear arms, cruel and unusual punishment, excessive bail, freedom of religion and of speech (political speech, especially), though Madison added the important Fifth Amendment which protects individuals from torture by exempting them from self-incrimination in legal testimony and guaranteeing "due process." Habeas Corpus protection was included (the English had passed such a law earlier, before the Glorious Revolution).

Both the American Declaration of Independence and the American Constitution reflect not only the spirit and the particulars of the English Bill of Rights, but also the general philosophies of government expressed by John Locke in his *Two Treatises*. Locke developed two key ideas: social contract and natural rights – both were taken up by Jefferson in the Declaration.

Locke, like others of his generation, had been strongly influenced by the discoveries in astronomy and physics by Isaac Newton and others. The medieval view of the cosmos had been shaken by the theories of such astronomers as Copernicus and Galileo, who asserted that the earth and other planets revolved around the sun, rather than the sun revolving around the earth (an ancient religious conviction supported by the Roman Catholic Church, which charged Galileo with heresy and imprisoned him for a time).

In an historic breakthrough, Newton proved that the planets orbited the sun by supplying laws of physics and mathematical formulas to back up his hypothesis. He was the Einstein of his time (late 1600s) and is still regarded as one of the most influential men in human history. As a result of Newton's discoveries, abetted by ongoing astronomical data and the founding of the Royal Society in London to oversee scientific advances and innovations, educated men and women began to see the cosmos as an orderly, clock-work creation, majestic in its size, disciplined movements, and adherence to laws of nature – laws humans could understand. It was a revelation. The universe was scientific in its nature – it was ruled by natural laws. It was but a step from this conviction to a similar one – human society might be ordered by natural laws, too. Natural laws in the human arena would be "natural rights." So argued Locke and others of his generation and after.

John Locke's natural rights included "life, liberty and property." Jefferson, writing almost a century later, would amend this slightly, in his Declaration, to "life, liberty and the pursuit of happiness." When asked by Benjamin Franklin what happened to property, Jefferson replied that it was included in "pursuit of happiness." Americans can readily see that their Declaration of Independence, their 1789 Constitution, and Madison's Bill of Rights (the first ten amendments to the Constitution) drew upon the social contract and natural rights theories of Locke and Rousseau and the separation of powers notions of Baron Montesquieu of France – all of these men were members of what has come to be known as "the Enlightenment," a European-wide movement toward reason and citizens' rights in the late 17th and 18th centuries.

The English had overthrown two kings (both from the same ruling family), first in the 1640s, then in the 1680s. English subjects in America would do likewise, rejecting King George

III in the 1770s. The long struggle for parliamentary autonomy and citizens' rights in England paid dividends, but at the same time, "absolute" monarchies were being maintained in France, Russia and other countries. The continent of Europe was taking a different course, which is why developments in England and her colonies were so important. As late as the early 1940s, most of Europe was ruled by dictators or kings – including Germany, Italy, Portugal, Spain, Hungary, Poland, Romania, Russia, and Yugoslavia. Japan was a virtual military dictatorship and most countries in Latin America, though free of colonial rule, were run by heavy-handed military juntas or corrupt ruling families that did not allow political opposition. Almost every other country in the world in the 1940s was a colonial possession, either of the Western powers or of the new fascist and Communist states – or of Japan.

Democracy, as we know it, has been rare and fragile throughout history. One of the reasons continental European countries are so top-heavy with government bureaucracies and so heavily taxed is the long tradition of statism that goes back to Louis XIV in France – and beyond. The long struggle to rein in the power of kings was not a feature of European life as it was in England, the glaring exception being brave little Holland (the Netherlands) which fought an eighty year war against autocratic Spain for its religious, commercial and political freedom. The Dutch model had an enduring influence on England and the two together strongly influenced the United States.

America was fortunate to have been born, politically and philosophically, in the 18th century, when the dominant view of nature was one of order and intelligent design. Less than a century later, a very different view of nature would develop in response to the research and writings of Charles Darwin, reflecting his investigations into evolutionary biology. Nature red in tooth and claw, the survival of the fittest, would inspire very different political movements – racist and fascist. The Nazi movement in the early 20th century would reflect Darwinian understandings (and misunderstandings) of nature and apply them to human nature and human society. Hitler's God was one who approved, not only of Hitler, but of the struggle of the fittest and the vanquishing of the weak. That this view was in perfect concert with the desire of the Nazis (mostly ex-soldiers) to re-fight World War I and make Germany a world power, added to its attraction.

The English Enlightenment, already in progress with Newton, whose masterwork, the *Principia Mathematica*, was published just before the Glorious Revolution, encompassed activities and discoveries in astronomy, physics and mathematics. This was not the only interesting coincidence in publishing dates: Adam Smith's bible of capitalism, *The Wealth of Nations*, was published in England the same year that Jefferson's *Declaration of Independence* was made public in America – 1776. Smith's book is an argument for the free market, suggesting that supply and demand will help set prices fairly and that self-interest, operating as a kind of "invisible hand," will help create a general good, despite that this was not overtly intended by the manufacturer or provider of goods and services. Smith's argument is directly in opposition to the command economies of socialist, fascist and Communist states in which central planning by bureaucrats anticipates general needs and guides markets. The unspoken truth about these authoritarian systems is that they also provide the power-hungry individual (the dictator and his cronies) with an excuse to seize the wealth-producing property of the nation. Not content with overbearing political control, they must control the economy, too – and control of culture and communications is not far behind (Orwell's *1984*). Nazi Germany, Soviet Russia, Imperial Japan, Communist North Korea, and Mao's China all tried "autarky," a closed system in which complete self-sufficiency was sought and open markets and convertibility of currencies rejected. When American authors visited Nazi Germany or Soviet Russia they had to spend their royalties there in local currency, which they couldn't take out of the country. Of course, few countries were rich enough in natural resources to achieve true autarky, so Hitler's Germany and Imperial Japan had to expand by seizing oil, foodstuffs and other commodities from their neighbors, whom they invaded. The greatest irony can be found in Imperial Japan's name for its erstwhile empire, "The Greater East-Asia Co-Prosperity Sphere." Seeking such an economic sphere (or common market) by force cost Japan over 2 million lives and devastated its armed forces and its great cities. After the war, Japan easily achieved just such a co-prosperity sphere, via Anglo-American free trade and democratic capitalism.

The Wealth of Nations was aimed against state monopolies dominated by royal governments of the time – an economic system known as mercantilism that did not allow free trade between sovereign nations and their own and other colonies. Americans, when declaring their liberties in 1776 were fighting not only for political freedom, but for economic freedom, which makes Smith's book very appropriate to that year of revolution.

The British Enlightenment was characterized by an explosion of the free press and the popularity of coffee house culture, especially in London – coffee houses being places where people could read the many new publications and freely argue politics, religion and economics. This phenomenon developed in the final decades of the 17th century, in tandem with the converging threads of the Glorious Revolution. The general approval of a free press was one of the many English folkways and characteristics carried over from Britain to the American colonies in the 1600s and 1700s.

The late Russell Kirk wrote a wonderful little book, *America's British Culture*, that should be required reading in American high schools and colleges. In four succinct chapters (chapters 2 through 5 in the 1993 edition), he laid out exactly how significant were Britain's contributions to American language and literature, law, representative government, and general morals and mores. His first chapter argues that there is a necessity for a general culture and that ours is and always has been Anglo-American. A final chapter is a broadside against multiculturalism, which Kirk, as a conservative, might be expected to loathe. In that regard, it is worthwhile to note that the liberal Democrat historian, Arthur Schlesinger, Jr., who worked for the election of John F. Kennedy and was rewarded with a position in his administration, also wrote a book attacking multiculturalism: *The Disuniting of America* (1991).

The American ties to Britain via language are obvious, with each nation's authors, novelists, poets and historians readily available on either side of the Atlantic, as the great showcases for live theater, London's West End and New York's Broadway, are in continual interchange of plays and musicals. The pop music and the movies of the two countries are interchangeable, too – and British and other English-speaking actors (from Australia, Canada, New Zealand, South Africa, even India) are regarded as welcome "stars" in the United States, brethren to America's homegrown actors and actresses, and equally qualified for Academy Awards. In terms of written language, no American sources have had as profound an influence in the United States as Shakespeare's plays and the King James Bible. Modern English, with many technical and other terms donated by America, has a vocabulary, as Kirk points out, of half a million words, far more than are found in any other European language. English is the dominant international language of science, air and other navigation, pop culture, the Internet, diplomacy, the European Union, NATO, and international business. Upwards of a billion people in the world can speak or read English and it is the second language in many countries and the most widely taught language on earth.

Britain's contributions to American law have been cited earlier, as have its contributions to representative government. Most religious denominations in the United States are derived from British originals, including the Congregational, Episcopal, Baptist, Methodist, and Presbyterian churches – and even the Salvation Army. As Kirk put it, a large Roman Catholic population notwithstanding, American Christianity has been British Christianity.

Kirk, like Alexis de Tocqueville more than a century earlier, identifies certain characteristically American attitudes: a relish for business, considerable personal independence, a puritanical streak, a tendency to live somewhat apart from others (farms, suburbs, exurbs), fascination with the law, utilitarianism and egalitarianism – and an enthusiasm for education, including the early – and often – founding of universities. He adds that, as the British were very taken with ancient Greece and Rome and trained their young men in the Greco-Roman classics (a policy that has, alas, eroded in recent decades), Americans, too looked back to the classical world not only for architectural models, but for models of government.

When Michael Hart wrote his book, *The 100*, a compendium of the 100 most influential persons who have ever lived (over a 5,000 year history), he placed more Britons on the list than persons from any other country. There were Americans, too – and some who had lived in both countries. The extraordinary accomplishments in science made by Britons (the list includes Newton, Watt, Faraday, Maxwell, Dalton, Bell, Fleming, Harvey, Rutherford, Lister, Jenner, and Francis Bacon – not to mention that turncoat Briton, Benjamin Franklin) contributed directly to the American interest in science and technology. America has dominated Nobel prizes since the Second World War and any list of inventors over the past three centuries is crowded with British and American names. Economists Thomas Malthus and Adam Smith are on Hart's list, too, along with John Locke, Thomas Jefferson and George Washington – the latter two being British subjects into middle age.

In many ways, America is a continuation of British civilization, but with a large door open to immigrants from other countries.

Though the French Revolution in the 1790s (*after* the American) seems the favorite of historians – and certainly the favorite of all authoritarian political figures from Napoleon to Marx to Lenin and Stalin, it was an abject failure, resulting in anarchy, mass killing, dictatorship and decades of war. The Glorious Revolution in England and the American Revolution a century later were much less bloody and resulted in peaceful and permanent progressive changes. They were surely the most successful revolutions in modern world history.

The liberal death wish mandates a pessimistic and dark view of both Britain and America. Admittedly, any Irish historian could easily compile a stinging indictment of Britain's treatment of Ireland – and many other places – over centuries. The British Empire was brutally established and brutally maintained. Famines killed millions in Ireland and India while they were subject to British colonial control – because British leadership was not vigorous or humane enough to address the crises. A micro view of life in England in the 17th and 18th centuries – and even the 19th century – would reveal terrible poverty and inequality, corrupt politics, heavy-handed censorship, a limited franchise, arrogant elites, major public health issues and the like – much of which made good story material for Charles Dickens. Desperately poor people could be hanged for a long list of offenses we would today regard as minor infractions. Society was dominated by an unforgiving class system.

Britain supported a slave trade from Africa to the Americas for centuries (though, with strong official Christian church support, it eventually outlawed slavery decades before America's Civil War). It also forced on China a trade in opium that ruined uncounted lives while making fortunes for a few. The British political elite treated its own people badly in many respects and tolerated a level of poverty and injustice we would today find repugnant and unconscionable. But so did France, Portugal, Spain and the Netherlands, all of which had world-wide empires. The sins of Britain were the sins of all, but the virtues of Britain (and her English-speaking colonies) were unique. American treatment of native Indians, like Australian treatment of native aborigines, was appalling. Yet both settlement groups quickly constructed modern, democratic, prosperous, scientifically advanced nations – which the native inhabitants had failed to do over a course of thousands of years. In more modern times, America's suppression of Filipinos in a brutal war in the early 1900s, and the entire Vietnam War were deplorable (as, it must be noted, were the murderous policies of North Vietnam's Communists, 1961-75).

But if one takes the macro view, it is obvious that what is at stake in the world today is the survival of these unique Anglo-American virtues. India has adopted the English style of parliamentary democracy. Most of the new states freed from colonial status in the half century after World War II have also adopted the parliamentary style of government. At least half of mankind lives in democratic countries, the highest proportion in history. Of the ten largest countries in the world, in terms of population, only two – Russia and China – are not free or partly free, according to Freedom House and others who rate levels of democracy around the world.

The Anglo-American contributions to democracy, the rule of law, human rights, science, technology, religion, literature, art and architecture, film and music, are extraordinary. This

vast cultural legacy – including, especially, political culture –
is now at risk.

POLITICAL PARTIES AND THE TRANSITION TO DEMOCRACY

The American Constitution established a republic, not a democracy. The Glorious Revolution established a constitutional monarchy in England, not a democracy. Both systems evolved into majority rule democracy in time – America sooner. The Americans, as noted, adopted a checks-and-balances form of government in which the Congress was meant to be the most powerful branch, with the courts least powerful. England was then moving toward more priority for parliament, but it took from the Glorious Revolution (1688-89) until the 1830s for parliament to emerge stronger than the monarch. It then took the better part of a century for the House of Commons branch of Parliament to supersede in power the more aristocratic and non-elected House of Lords. This happened in 1911, when the king threw his political support behind the House of Commons. Such a remarkable change has never happened in America. But the Americans, leaving voting laws up to the states, were granting voting rights to all males half a century before Britain or France. Early in the 20th century, both nations extended the franchise to women. Securing voting rights for African-Americans in the South took another half century.

In a sense, the first Anglo political party was that of the landed barons who forced King John to sign the Magna Carta in 1215. Self-interested groups who opposed kings in England were "parties" of sorts, with landed interests doing so for centuries, joined by the church, then by banking, financial and industrial interests later. Landed parties tended to coalesce into the Tory group by 1700 or so, and financial/industrial interests coalesced into the Whig Party, whose religious piety and business orientation strongly influenced the Whig Party in America. Out of the two contending parties in Britain in the 18th century would emerge a reform party of the *noblesse oblige* variety, the Liberal Party in the 19th century, whose most respected leadership figure was William Gladstone, elected Prime Minister four times. Not only the reformers, but nearly all politicians in these parties were wealthy or privileged. Only much later (around 1900) would a party emerge in England with working class, blue collar members of Parliament – the Labor Party.

It is not easy to trace present day parties back to those early parties and that is true of America, too. In some ways today's Republican Party is a direct descendant of the pre-Civil War American Whigs, but in other ways, it resembles the Whigs' rival, the Democratic Party of Andrew Jackson – and both modern American parties can find some inspiration in the "Republican" party of Thomas Jefferson as it emerged around 1800.

The American Founding Fathers did not anticipate political parties and made little provision for them. That was understandable in that at the same hour parties in England were vague and shapeless. The sharply delineated political parties of England, along with the cabinet form of government led by a strong prime minister, were just beginning to develop with Robert Walpole as head of the cabinet in the early 1700s. In the United States, the founding Federalist Party, which included George Washington, John Adams and Alexander Hamilton, was opposed by Thomas Jefferson, whose party – winner of the 1800 presidential election – has been variously described by historians as "anti-Federalist," "Jeffersonian," "Democratic-Republican," or simply, "Republican."

The Federalists believed in a strong central government, the industrial and urban development of America, a limited franchise, and rule by educated elites – all of which they passed on to their successors, the American Whigs. The new Whig Party, in turn, strongly identified with Britain's Whigs in terms of pro-business policies, Protestant religious piety, middle class norms, peace and prosperity. In addition, American Whigs were lukewarm about territorial expansion through war, the extension of slavery, and frontier equality. They took a dim view of heavy immigration, supported temperance movements, and backed state laws that attempted to discipline sexuality. They were rather like Republicans in the 1950s.

The Whig vision, as it turned out, was more realistic than the Jeffersonian vision of a nation of 100 million farmers. America did industrialize and eventually overtake the Industrial Revolution's leader, Great Britain. America's future was urban and industrial, as the Federalists had hoped. Like the Federalists, the Whigs urged government subsidies for certain business ventures, including canal-building and railroad projects.

Today, it is the Democrats who have adopted some of the Federalist-Whig program – a strong central bank, a strong central government, rule by elites. But the Democrats also continue some of the attitudes of Andrew Jackson's rough-and-tumble Democratic Party: strong support for immigration, raffish individualism, and religious pluralism. The Jacksonian Democrats were also strong supporters of free enterprise, Indian removal, and of slavery. Many Whigs eventually joined the new Republican Party of the 1860s, which was anti-slavery. One of them was Abraham Lincoln.

Today's Democratic Party underwent a sea change toward big government and higher taxes during the presidencies of Woodrow Wilson, Franklin Roosevelt and Lyndon Johnson (a political culture promoted today by Barack Obama). Republicans today assert some of the localism, low taxes and free market attitudes of the Jacksonian Democrats. In other words, both parties have a scrambled past, but many Whiggish attitudes, especially in regard to business, Protestant cultural norms, expansion of education, limited government, and loyalty to the original Anglo-American culture and Anglo-European ethnicity, prevail among today's Republicans. Since the McGovern era and the Vietnam War, Democrats have become increasingly socialist, isolationist, and opposed to the original founding Anglo-American culture described by Kirk in *America's British Culture*.

Whigs and Republicans maintained ties with Britain, as did Democrats, beginning with Grover Cleveland and Woodrow Wilson. World War I, World War II and the Cold War cemented the alliance between the two largest English-speaking countries regardless of which party held the White

House. But the cross-Atlantic ties began earlier. Walter Russell Mead, in his excellent study, *God and Gold*, details how a maritime model for international capitalism was established first by the Dutch (a little appreciated historical fact), then adopted by the English, and finally copied by their English-speaking cousins, the Americans.

As Britain moved toward the free trade model of Adam Smith, the British navy and merchant marine (each the largest on earth) were creating a safe haven for American ships and American trade. In a sense, the United States was sheltered within a larger system while Britain poured investment capital into the U.S. and Europe poured in cheap labor via immigration. The result, sheltered by ever-changing tariffs, was an American boom that propelled America to industrial first place in the world by the 1890s, a position it has held ever since.

Beyond that and despite occasional frictions, Britain and America settled boundary claims along the Canadian border and opened one another's markets (manufactured goods from Britain to America, raw materials and foodstuffs from America to Britain). Free trade was strongly supported by Gladstone, who was a political model and a hero to an American college student named Woodrow Wilson. English and American leaders had seen to the triumph of Adam Smith over mercantilism.

The two countries also shared much in the cultural and political sphere. There had been a strong anti-slavery movement in both England and New England. Britain's civil service inspired one in America. The Boy Scout movement migrated from Britain to America.

One big difference between the two countries was that America had a written constitution and Britain didn't. This has contributed, as noted, to the reality that America's written constitution is liable to interpretation by courts, while courts in Britain cannot overthrow laws of Parliament and do not enjoy the sweeping powers (including the illegal power to legislate) that American federal judges exercise.

The American Constitution is simple and limited – or it is supposed to be. An important point to be made about it is that it is, philosophically, a compromise between Enlightenment optimism, based on confidence in human rationality, and Protestant-Calvinist pessimism about human nature. Political movements that have proceeded on a belief in the natural goodness of man (derived in part from the optimism of Rousseau and Locke) have floundered on the inherent evil in man – his greed, appetite for power, cruelty and selfishness. Rationally based revolutions have failed because they cast aside institutions in society (churches, labor unions, political parties, newspapers and other media) that put a check on the state. Revolutionary France, Soviet Russia and Nazi Germany all turned nightmarish as the state took control of everything or almost everything and there were no checks and balances on those who ran the state.

The American Constitution, by contrast, acknowledges on its first page the inherent wickedness in humans by providing immediately a mechanism for impeaching and removing from office wayward presidents and members of the federal courts (the House would indict, the Senate convict). Also upfront is the unusual rule that the first class of senators would serve only two years, the second class four and the third class (and all following classes) six. This staggered arrangement for the U.S. Senate meant that only a third of the Senate would be up for election every two years, along with the entire House of Representatives. Consequently, for a dangerous or revolutionary political movement to capture the Senate it would take two or three election cycles to reach a majority, by which time the fanaticism of the movement may have run its course.

There is a deep distrust of human nature in the U.S. Constitution, but there is also a soaring optimism about republican self-government, derived from the Enlightenment – which had provided the Founding Fathers with a belief in both the social contract and the inherent natural rights of humans. As a result, a sensible balance was struck between optimism and pessimism. Calvinist Protestantism, which was the dominant influence in most British-American religious denominations, including even the Anglican-Episcopal churches, was a good antidote to the men-are-inherently-good ideas of Locke and Rousseau. As a wise person once remarked, anyone who has raised a child knows that humans are not inherently good. The Calvinists believed not only that most children were inherently bad, but that most people were destined to hell. Thus the shotgun marriage between Calvinism and the English Enlightenment proved sensible and long lasting.

The Founding Fathers wanted Congress to have most of the power, with a president in second place, indirectly elected by the state legislatures (via an electoral college). The courts were a distant third. Today we have an imperial president (often a rank amateur – like Carter or Obama), a runaway court and a weak Congress that is largely a congeries of special interests. The Founding Fathers sensibly anticipated that at times the president might be out of control and have to be impeached and removed from office, that at times Congress could become irresponsible and be subject to the president's multiple vetoes, and that at times the courts could overstep their boundaries and judges would then face impeachment and removal. The discipline of impeachment, as we can see, has not been exercised often enough by our soft, weak Congresses.

Despite the fact that Britain and America have had somewhat different political systems, they have found common cause in modern times and have stood together in numerous world-shaking wars – to the good of mankind.

ANGLO-AMERICAN COOPERATION IN THREE WORLD WARS AND THE ANGLO-AMERICAN NEW WORLD ORDER

Oddly missing from most school history textbooks, as a theme, is the great story of the 20th Century – the triumph of the democracies over Imperial Germany, Nazi Germany, Imperial Japan and Soviet Russia. Victory for the English-speaking democracies in the titanic struggles we know as World War I, World War II and the Cold War is the dominant theme of the 20th Century. Textbook authors, often people who under-appreciate democracy or who mourn the fact that socialism did not, in the end, triumph in the industrial world, miss the point entirely and mislead their readers. Any sensible person who looks at the slavery Nazi Germany imposed on a host of countries, the mass murder of millions by Hitler, Mao and Stalin, the killing fields of Cambodia, or even the somewhat lesser atrocities of Castro's social-fascist dictatorship for half a century in Cuba (robbing Cubans of political, intellectual and personal freedom – and any modicum of prosperity), is bound to conclude that the English-speaking countries, after much sacrifice in lives and treasure, managed to save Western Europe – the heartland of

Western Civilization – from totalitarianism, and at the same time save themselves and much of the world from a similar fate.

This should be especially appreciated by the overcivilized, the libertines and libertarians who enjoy extraordinary personal rights and freedoms in the urban Western world but who seem unable to acknowledge it. They would have been the first headed to the Gulags and death camps of the totalitarians. Yet they are the least in appreciation for the sacrifices of their fellow citizens on their behalf – sacrifices that are ongoing in a dangerous world.

President Woodrow Wilson, inspired by the internationalism of Gladstone, stayed out of World War I until he saw that a victory for Kaiser's Germany would be a disaster for Britain and America. Gradually, his instinct to reform at home grew into a vision for reform on a global stage. Wilson, an intellectual and an idealist, became convinced that America could swing the tide in the war in favor of the democracies (at that time, April, 1917, even Russia was nominally a democracy, though not for long). Wilson felt the sacrifices in lives were worth it if after the war a just peace could be concluded and a League of Nations established to maintain the peace. His outlook was naïve, as we can see in retrospect, for he envisioned a kind of world parliament, in which each country had one vote. A very small country would have equal weight with a large, powerful one – a fact noted without approval by Franklin Roosevelt, who was Assistant Secretary of the Navy under Wilson.

As a consequence of this idealistic outlook, Wilson could claim that World War I was a war to end all wars. Unfortunately for Wilson, he travelled to Europe without Republican colleagues and did not carefully establish bipartisan support for his League and for other aspects of the peace treaty following the defeat of Germany in November, 1918. As a result, the Republicans defeated the treaty (including membership in the League) in the U.S. Senate and Wilson went on a campaign by train to convince the American people to put pressure on the Senate to accept the League and the Versailles Treaty, as it was known. His health broke, he suffered a devastating stroke and his presidency sank into oblivion. Wilson was a great failure in the White House, but he had a powerful vision, one taken up a generation later by another Democrat, Franklin D. Roosevelt.

Kaiser Wilhelm of Germany had a master plan for Europe that shared some aspects of the one later adopted by Adolf Hitler. Had he won the war, the Kaiser would have annexed portions of neighboring countries and would have forced much of Europe into an economic union dominated by Germany. The Reich would have become a geographical and economic giant, a superpower – though nothing like the Canada-sized monstrosity Hitler envisioned as his Third Reich. This would have violated Britain's centuries-old dictum that no single nation should be allowed to dominate Europe (or, if hostile, control the Channel ports).

Britain's devotion to this principle, backed by the United States, explains in broad terms the wars against Kaiser Germany, Hitler Germany and the long Cold War with Soviet Russia. Germany and Russia, like Napoleonic France long before, were prevented by British-American arms from dominating all of Europe. Especially crucial was the 11-month military campaign that began on D-Day, the sixth of June,

1944, which prevented both Hitler and Stalin from long term control of Western Europe, the more industrialized, and densely populated portion of Europe – and the heartland of ancient and Medieval Western Civilization.

The Cold War, 1945-91, was a long, exhausting struggle against an over-armed, belligerent Soviet Russia dominated by Leninist Communists. Britain and America each maintained large land armies, massive air and naval forces, and nuclear weapons in Western Europe to protect West Germany (including West Berlin), France, Italy and other countries threatened by the Soviets. To the surprise of liberals and country club Republicans (though not Ronald Reagan), Soviet-imposed Communism in Eastern Europe collapsed in 1989 and the Soviet Union itself dissolved in 1991. Former Secretary of State, Henry Kissinger – an establishment Republican – had worked for detente with the Soviets, including surrender of our military superiority – because the Soviets were here to stay. Prize-winning economists in the West said that the Soviet economy was sound in the 1980s, at the very time it was collapsing. Reagan was ridiculed for saying, early in his presidency in a speech before the British Parliament, that the Soviet Union and Communism were unnatural and would end up on the ash heap of history. He was right, of course, a fact graciously admitted later by Kissinger in his memoir of the period, *Diplomacy* (1994).

Wilson's vision collapsed and his League of Nations, without the U.S. as a member, was incapable of keeping the peace. Dictators simply withdrew from the League, built for war, and went to war – a pattern we are seeing again today with countries leaving the UN Nonproliferation Treaty, building nuclear weapons, and perhaps using them in the future. Wilson failed, but Franklin Roosevelt took up his cause during World War II, beginning with the Atlantic Charter, agreed upon by Winston Churchill in a wartime visit to North America. Though the U.S. was not yet in the war (August, 1941), the two principal English-speaking countries agreed on several points as war aims, including self-determination (democracy), freedom of the seas, free trade, and an "association of nations" that would, by 1942, go by the name United Nations. Most of the eight points of the Atlantic Charter were solidly in keeping with the maritime global system of Gladstone and others who supported England's version of the Dutch model for world trade. An Anglo-American "new world order" was emerging and would become reality as a result of two wartime conferences on American soil, the Breton Woods Conference in July, 1944, and the Dumbarton Oaks Conference in August, 1944. The former had over 700 delegates from 45 countries (just about all the free countries in the world) meeting to set up a world financial system which included the World Bank, the International Monetary Fund and an exchange rate system for world currencies that evolved later into the General Agreement on Trade and Tariffs (GATT). Despite controversy and some problems, these institutions survive today and Communist China and post-Communist Russia had to meet their standards and regulations in order to participate in world trade. The U.S. dollar has been the mainstay currency of the new system.

At Dumbarton Oaks, 45 nations agreed to create the UN (though the term had been in use for a few years at that point). The first meeting of the new UN was planned for

San Francisco in 1945. Wilson's parliament of nations had reappeared, with one important change – a Security Council. And this time the United States would not only join the new league of nations, it would permanently host it in New York.

If one takes a micro view of Anglo-American relations, even during the great wars, there is plenty of evidence of backbiting, resentments, selfishness (especially on the part of the United States) and ill will between military and other leaders. But this account is belied by the macro view which clearly shows, on the record, that the shared price paid for the Anglo-American New World Order was high. In World War I Britain suffered some 700,000 deaths, a staggering toll brought to over a million when U.S. and Commonwealth deaths are included. In World War II, again, about a million English-speaking citizens died, with hundreds of thousands of others maimed, blinded or crippled for life.

In his D-Day speech on the radio, framed as a prayer and addressed to "Almighty God," Franklin Roosevelt told the nation that "our sons, pride of our nation," had embarked on "a mighty endeavor" on behalf of "our Republic, our religion and our civilization." FDR had the prayer/address bound in leather and sent to Winston Churchill. Today's political correctness cranks would be hysterical at a presidential address presented as a prayer and would reject any mention of "our religion" (America is not a Christian nation, Barack Obama famously said). They would also argue that our civilization is no better than any other. So far have we come since Roosevelt's time.

What was at stake in the mighty struggles of the 20th century is scarcely acknowledged by many in the intelligentsia.

Churchill himself had begun a history of the English-speaking peoples, but World War II interrupted his work and the four volumes were not published until the 1950s. His work went up to about 1900, thus leaving out the 20th Century. More recently, a British historian, Andrew Roberts, has written an excellent account of the 20th Century, *A History of the English Speaking Peoples Since 1900*, thus filling out the effort begun by Churchill. Andrews leaves no doubt that the three world wars were the key events of the century and that they were three of the four major challenges to the English-speaking people – the fourth challenge being that of Islamic terrorism.

In tandem with the new axis of dictators, fundamentalist Islamic terrorism poses a serious threat to the English-speaking countries and other democracies. FDR was right when he said that "our civilization" was at stake. It is again today.

EPILOGUE

Franklin Roosevelt approved of Woodrow Wilson's idea of a parliament of nations, but unlike Wilson, he understood that a parliament of large and small countries was an unrealistic decision-making body. FDR, a pragmatist with a keen sense of where the real power lay in any political situation, decided that the great powers of the day should have sway over any league of nations. Consequently, he decided that the new body, the United Nations, would have a Security Council made up of the great powers (each of which would have a veto) and this would be separate from the General Assembly, which would be a debating forum. He chose the two great industrial powers of the day, America and Soviet Russia, as permanent members, along with the two countries with the largest overseas empires, Great Britain and France. Then he added China – a poor, weak, war-ravaged country, but one whose eventual power and influence he was wise enough to foresee. China, of course, at that time, was not yet Communist.

FDR can be accused of being naïve in thinking that a paranoid mass murderer like Stalin would ever favor anything but self interest. Roosevelt was used to dealing with ward heelers, big city machine politicians and tough labor leaders –

men far removed from the genteel circles he had lived in most of his life. But these tough men were a far cry from the sadistic butcher, Stalin, responsible for the deaths of millions in his own country, including his own faithful followers and fellow Bolsheviks.

Nevertheless, FDR's vision applies today with a certain irrefutable accuracy. FDR correctly forecast, in a memorable phrase, that the Soviet Union would eventually fly apart like a cracked plate. He also knew that the U.S. was working on an atomic bomb, a project he personally gave the green light to – and he knew the Germans were also working on such a project and must have guessed that the Russians were, too. From the perspective of nuclear weapons, the great powers, however much they may distrust or even hate one another, have an equal interest in preventing nuclear war. A nuclear war today would not only permanently damage the planet, but it would derail the world economy. This would send Communist China into a deep economic depression that might result in internal turmoil, perhaps even a revolution that might topple the regime. Russia's economy would sink, too, if international trade collapses. The number one target in any nuclear war, besides Israel, would be the United States. With its $16 trillion economy, the U.S. is the lynchpin of the world economy. If the world economy staggers, hundreds of millions might starve in Africa and India, Pakistan and Bangladesh. The world would be in a crisis never seen before. Why, then, do China and Russia not work to avoid nuclear war instead of actually facilitating it? Economic warfare must replace military warfare or the planet and its inhabitants may suffer irreparable damage. Russia and China, like post-war

Germany and Japan, are well suited to economic warfare – as we are. Economic blockades and pressures can disarm the new Axis countries. It is not yet too late.

Poor leadership in the West, as noted in earlier chapters, has been a prime reason the world is drifting toward catastrophe. The last three weak American presidents – one smart but weak, one stronger but not so smart, and one a naive leftist – have brought us to the edge. Americans elected a part-time school teacher as president in 2008. Earlier, Jimmy Carter's sole preparation for being CEO of the world's greatest nation was a four-year stint as governor of Georgia. Voters knew as little about him as they did of Bill Clinton, governor for ten years of a minor, politically corrupt inland state, or of Barack Obama, who had been in the Senate but four years and had no other genuine credentials. George W. Bush had been governor of Texas for a few years, but even that honor would have eluded him if his father's name had not been Bush. Hillary Clinton would never have been elected to the U.S. Senate from New York had she not been married to Bill Clinton. None of these people, including Hillary, were good presidential material. With leaders like these, we are in deep trouble.

The U.S. Congress has also been a bust, which is why public approval ratings of Congress are generally below 20 per cent. The steps outlined in chapter one would help elevate better people at party nominating conventions. Downgrading the primaries is a must, and looking to governors, rather than members of Congress, may be a better way to go. A strong governor in the FDR or Reagan mold might rise to the challenges, especially if willing to countenance a strong secretary of state. Governors tend to be up on domestic issues and usually have a better feel for fiscal responsibility than members of Congress, but they often lack experience in the international arena (Rick Perry being a case in point). Presidents since Kennedy have tended to want to be their own secretaries of state, with grievous results. Presidents like Eisenhower and Truman had strong secretaries of state, with better results. A very able governor, like Mitt Romney, Jon Huntsman or Chris Christie, with a strong secretary of state, could cope with the dreadful problems at hand.

Put with brutal frankness, the survival of the U.S. and the other English-speaking democracies is not guaranteed. It will require strong, enlightened leadership, reflecting active citizen participation in the processes of finding and elevating leaders – and holding them accountable. A continuing libertarian vacation from such participation will be self-destructive.

Yet there is reason for hope. Economic growth in India, Africa, Brazil and other previously disadvantaged areas of the world is strong. If the trillions of dollars wasted on armaments can be diverted to fighting hunger, disease and poverty world-wide, the human race could make a quantum leap into relative peace and prosperity. The "Arab Spring" (and demands for democracy in Russia and other places lacking it), bodes well. People want normal lives and a better situation for their children. Governments should take a version of the Hippocratic oath: first, do no harm. The great democracies should apply unrelenting pressure on dictatorships, psychological pressure that undermines their legitimacy, as Western Europe's democracies undermined the Soviet Union and its brutal puppet regimes in Eastern

Europe in the decades following the Second World War.

The modern world does not have to face death. If democracy triumphs in Iran, Russia, Syria, Venezuela, Cuba and other countries deprived of it – and China avoids the mistakes made by an earlier rising power, Kaiser Germany, the people of the world will share the solid expectation of enjoying freedom and prosperity far into the future. The model for that freedom and prosperity is available from the democratic family of nations today. Only a handful of authoritarian states threaten that future. They must not be allowed to succeed.

President Franklin Roosevelt and Prime Minister Winston Churchill met in August, 1941, in Canada (before Pearl Harbor) and worked up the joint declaration known to history as the Atlantic Charter. The document served as a basis for later policies, including economic ones. It offered a global view that would have pleased Adam Smith, William Gladstone and Woodrow Wilson, combining typical Anglo-American ideals: freedom of the seas; the disarmament of aggressor states; lowered tariffs moving toward free trade; the advancement of democracy and self-government; and freedom from fear and want (the latter borrowed from FDR's famous Four Freedoms speech earlier that year – he had also included freedom of worship and freedom of speech).

These ideals served the world well in the last struggle against an axis of dictators. They will serve equally well today against a new axis of dictators.

THE AUTHOR

Paul J. Delmont, PhD, is a journalist and historian published in *Financial Times, USA Today, The Weekly Standard, The Daily Caller, The Saturday Evening Post* and several top fifty American newspapers, including the *Omaha World-Herald,* the *Baltimore Sun,* the *New Orleans Times-Picayune* and the *Minneapolis Star-Tribune.* He has extensive teaching experience at the university level and is a member of the National Book Critics Circle.

www.thegreatliberaldeathwish.com